INTRODUCTION TO SPEECHWORK FOR ACTORS

INTRODUCTION TO SPEECHWORK FOR ACTORS

An Inclusive Approach

RON CARLOS

SERIES EDITOR: BILL CONNINGTON

methuen | drama
LONDON • NEW YORK • OXFORD • NEW DELHI • SYDNEY

METHUEN DRAMA
Bloomsbury Publishing Plc
50 Bedford Square, London, WC1B 3DP, UK
1385 Broadway, New York, NY 10018, USA
29 Earlsfort Terrace, Dublin 2, Ireland

BLOOMSBURY, METHUEN DRAMA and the Methuen Drama
logo are trademarks of Bloomsbury Publishing Plc

First published in Great Britain 2023

Copyright © Ron Carlos, 2023

Series Preface © Bill Connington, 2023

Ron Carlos has asserted his right under the Copyright,
Designs and Patents Act, 1988, to be identified as author of this work.

Series design by Charlotte Daniels
Cover image © Troyek / iStock Photo

All rights reserved. No part of this publication may be reproduced
or transmitted in any form or by any means, electronic or mechanical,
including photocopying, recording, or any information storage or
retrieval system, without prior permission in writing from the publishers.

Bloomsbury Publishing Plc does not have any control over, or responsibility
for, any third-party websites referred to or in this book. All internet addresses
given in this book were correct at the time of going to press. The author
and publisher regret any inconvenience caused if addresses have changed
or sites have ceased to exist, but can accept no responsibility
for any such changes.

A catalogue record for this book is available from the British Library.

A catalog record for this book is available from the Library of Congress.

ISBN: HB: 978-1-3501-4595-5
       PB: 978-1-3501-4596-2
       ePDF: 978-1-3501-4597-9
       eBook: 978-1-3501-4598-6

Series: Acting Essentials | AE

Typeset by Integra Software Services Pvt. Ltd.

To find out more about our authors and books visit www.bloomsbury.com
and sign up for our newsletters.

For all my teachers,

most of whom were my students,

and for Mishy

CONTENTS

List of figures x
List of tables xi
Foreword by Dawn-Elin Fraser xii
Series preface xiv
Acknowledgments xvi

Introduction 1
Assumptions and -isms 6
How to use this book 7
The International Phonetic Alphabet 8
Accent, dialect, and idiolect 9

1 **A snapshot of you** 11
Storytelling and conversation 11
Reading 12
Playing with sentence structures 13
Word lists 14

2 **Meet your text** 17
Some useful grammar concepts before we begin 18
Analyzing the text 21

3 **Language of your body** 35
Lexicon 35
Packaging your images 37
Word soaking 39

4 Color me aware 47
5 The work of awareness 59
Release 60
Isolate 67
Activate 81

6 The shape of your sound 87
7 Your own kind of music 91
Syllables 94
Word stress 96
Thought stress 97
Rhythm 97
Pitch 103
Pace 105
Volume 108

8 River of sounds 111
Jumping in the river 113
Vowel chart 115
Diphthongs 120
Lexical sets 121
Vowel phonetics 124

9 Splashing in the river 141
Plosives 143
Taps 150
Nasals 151
Trills 157
Fricatives 158
Affricates 165
Approximants 167
Lateral fricatives 170
Lateral approximants 172
Syllabic consonants 175
"R" roundup 176

10 Moving forward 187
    Strengthening your idiolect 187
    Visiting your sources 188
    Changing your speech 189
    Continuing your speechwork 191

Appendices
    A Daily practice template 193
    B Dialect breakdown template 194
    C Practice for consonant clusters 206
    D List of companion videos 212

Glossary 213
Bibliography 220

FIGURES

1 The skull and jaw 51
2 Muscles of the face 53
3 The larynx 55
4 The vocal tract and articulators 57
5 IPA chart 111

All illustrations by Frank Sansone

TABLES

1 Social Location 16
2 Idiolect Lexicon 36
3 Vocal Tract Posture 88
4 Vocal Tract Posture of My Idiolect 90
5 Phonemic Inventory of Vowels 122
6 Idiolectsploration of Sibilants 161
7 Fricative Clusters 163
8 Idiolectsploration of "L" 173
9 Idiolectsploration of Consonant "R" 178

FOREWORD

Hello there! I know we haven't met, but if you're holding *Introduction to Speechwork for Actors* in your hand, I'm excited for you, for you are about to begin an adventure. Aren't adventures exciting? They give us the opportunity to explore new territory, discover new ways of doing things (and thinking about them), and to learn a bit about ourselves along the way. I would imagine that if you've chosen this book (or had a very thoughtful professor choose it for you) the world of acting and theater are of interest to you. Like many students before you, you are about to discover (or are in the midst of discovering) that the most interesting of adventures don't require us to travel far from home but to journey within ourselves, paying attention to what draws our attention.

The trickiest thing about a new adventure can be figuring out how to start. After all, since we can't know what we don't know, how can we order our steps toward the knowledge that will fill in the blanks? The Speech adventure is an unusual one. We all communicate (and most of us speak) so we may wonder what exactly it is we need to be working on? In times past, there was a desire for a uniformity of speech. Called by many names—American Theater Standard, Transatlantic speech—this uniformity has fallen out of favor as more scripts are asking for a more diverse group of actors to play all sorts of roles. And thank goodness for that! It's an exciting moment for young actors who are being asked more and more to use themselves in their work. There is still, however, the desire to activate the language with specificity and to allow our curiosity to expand our options for each character we play. In other words, wouldn't it be thrilling to feel like your authentic self while using language to support choices both inside and outside your sphere of experience?

FOREWORD

The adventure that you've chosen to embark upon by choosing this book will allow you to do all of those things. With the unmatchable help, expertise, and humor of Ron Carlos, you'll be guided through all that language and speech have to offer. I've seen him work this magic with students from the undergraduate level (we trained together to become Certified Teachers of Knight-Thompson Speechwork) to some of the best graduate acting training programs in the country (we also taught together at the Yale School of Drama). He's worked extensively in theater, film, and television. Now he's bringing his considerable experience straight to you.

As with some of the greatest adventures, the stops along the way often lead us to the greatest of discoveries: that everything we needed for our journey was with us all along. This is my wish for you as you dive into this text with Ron as your guide. As you learn more about your instrument, text analysis, phonetic theory, and even accent work, may you find your curiosity awakened, your confidence built, and your acting work elevated. As you are drawn to pay attention to yourself, may it allow you to build awareness of the world around you and all that it has to offer. I'm so grateful to Ron for taking the care and time to create this marvelous resource. I cannot wait to introduce it to my students. And I cannot wait for you to embark on your great speech and language adventure!

Dawn-Elin Fraser
Associate Arts Professor, NYU
Head of Spoken Voice and Speech
New Studio on Broadway, Tisch School of the Arts

SERIES PREFACE

Acting Essentials is the first book series specifically intended for undergraduate students of drama. The books in the series are not theoretical; rather, they are practical. Fifty percent of the text consists of exercises designed to help the reader learn the material and apply it directly to rehearsals, auditions, and performances.

The series is comprehensive and aims to cover everything the undergraduate needs to know about performance. Classical and contemporary acting, acting for the camera, voice, speech, the business of acting, musical theater, and the Alexander Technique are all foundational topics for any acting program.

The books are also designed to speak to a large and diverse group of students. Diversity and inclusion are necessary because our world is diverse. Drama students come from all kinds of backgrounds and points of view, and so do the Acting Essentials authors. Moreover, the series is designed to remove geographic barriers to top-level instruction in drama. In the past, students often needed to study in New York, Los Angeles, or London to be able to work with well-known experts in the field. Acting Essentials makes the knowledge of those experts available to all students, regardless of where they study.

The Acting Essentials authors are highly experienced and respected. They are teachers and chairs of departments, but they are also practitioners—actors, directors, and writers. They speak their truths from a deep and deeply known place. Their voices are friendly, supportive, constructive, and enlightening. In essence, they have written workbooks that will show you the nuts and bolts of the acting craft. When craft is mastered, art can bloom.

To begin the study of acting is exciting and sometimes daunting. There is so much to learn—where to begin? The authors of Acting Essentials

SERIES PREFACE

speak with authoritative guidance, ready to pass their knowledge to succeeding generations. While building on the great traditions of the past, they are firmly rooted in contemporary artistry.

Studying acting is a journey, both into a new field of endeavor and into the self. This two-pronged journey is both outwardly and inwardly directed. Acting Essentials will lay the foundation for this lifelong journey, from the first flicker of intention all the way through the challenges of the professional world.

To quote the great Nigerian novelist Chinua Achebe, "There is no story that is not true." The Acting Essentials series is here to help every actor tell truthful stories.

Bill Connington, series editor

ACKNOWLEDGMENTS

It truly takes a village to make a book, especially during a global pandemic. Sending my gratitude to all of my friends and colleagues for the hand they played in this project.

To all of my colleagues at or formerly at Methuen Drama: Dr. Aanchal Vij, Sam Nicholls, Meredith Benson, and especially Anna Brewer for your guidance, patience, and faith as this book moved from inception to publication.

To Eileen Chetti and Dawn Cunneen for their keen expertise.

To my production manager Amy Brownbridge, project manager Deborah Maloney and the production team at Integra for their work moving my manuscript through the works.

To literary agent Barbara Clark.

To my wonderful collaborator Frank Sansone for his brilliant anatomy illustrations and limitless patience for revision.

To my colleagues at the Yale School of Drama, especially Beth McGuire and Walton Wilson for helping me spread my wings as a teacher.

To my colleagues who read parts of this book and offered their generous feedback: Ashleigh Reade, Jeremy Sortore, Lee Nishri-Howitt, Eliza Simpson.

To Dawn-Elin Fraser, for being the best speech camp friend a boy could ask for.

To my teachers and mentors Nancy Houfek, Catherine Fitzmaurice, Daniel Diego Pardo, Jeff Morrison, Barbara Adrian, Andrew Wade, Andrea Caban, Phil Thompson.

To Edith Skinner, Arthur Lessac, Dudley Knight, Cicely Berry, and Kristin Linklater.

To all of the students who demanded creativity instead of tradition.

ACKNOWLEDGMENTS

To Micheila Jacobson, who read and attempted each exercise and taught me how to be better from two time zones away.

To Bill Connington, who believed in my work before I did and who came to the rescue every time I needed it. I could not have done this without your constant support.

And especially to Ricardo Pérez González for the gift of sweet "Stella Starchild" and for keeping all my pieces together while everything was scary and hard.

INTRODUCTION

A character in a play or screenplay is nothing but black ink, or maybe pixels, on a white page. A writer dreamed up a world, filled it with imaginary circumstances, and populated it with characters who have things to say. The writer's job is to take their dream world with limitless possibilities and confine it to what can be captured by ink and paper or pixels and light. The script then goes out to a group of collaborators who dream up the rest. As one of those collaborators, an actor, the barest minimum of your job is to say the words in the right order and stand where you're told. The bare minimum is already a lot of work. You, however, have chosen to move beyond the bare minimum by studying the art form. As an actor-artist, you have the opportunity to fill in the humanity of one or more of the characters in the writer's dreamworld. You are what can give the black marks on the white page breath and body, needs and sensation.

To inhabit the writer's world fully, you'll learn how to analyze a script for clues about what the world is like, who the characters are, what they need, and when they might be changed by the next turn of events. You'll learn about physicality and all the ways it informs us of our emotional temperature through sensation. You could learn to free up your artistic impulses from the mire of insecurity by studying clown. You'll study your voice and how to care for a healthy instrument capable of translating those impulses into sound that reveals the sensations of your body. And you'll learn about speech—the imperfect way we try to organize all the information gathered in our body and breath into sense.

One way to think about speech is what was once called elocution—dutifully pronouncing words "correctly" so an audience has a clear understanding of their meaning. As an actor-artist, however, you have the opportunity to transform your speech into something more. You have the power to move beyond speaking the words correctly and in the right order. People choose their words or blurt them before they even have the time to choose. Either way, those words have a purpose. You'll learn how to analyze the language your characters use, find the twists and turns, and search for clues about the intentions behind the words. As an actor-artist, you'll learn to make a writer's words mean something that can't be found in a dictionary. You can imbue the words with context from your own experiences and marry that context to your character's imaginary circumstances. You'll also learn about the sounds that you actually use in your day-to-day life to fulfill your own needs. Speaking is the way we turn our voice, tuned to the nuances of our emotional lives, into sense. At least we try. When you have a sense of how you use speech to meet your needs in the real world, you can use those skills to meet the needs of your character in the writer's world.

I fell in love with speech for what I now consider the wrong reasons. I was drawn to speech training as a young actor because I really wanted to hide myself. As a young gay man from the Midwest-sounding part of upstate New York, I felt that the way I spoke would keep me from getting all the jobs—and I wanted all the jobs. I loved learning how my mouth worked and how sounds were created; I loved changing my speech sounds to not sound like me. Despite pronouncing things perfectly, I was still sometimes unintelligible. In graduate school, I learned how to analyze language and I loved understanding all the little bits of the text and what they meant. It was a eureka moment for me—I could perfect the sounds and speak the texts with perfect sense! But something was still missing. I was a rigid actor. I couldn't respond to the many unplanned events that happen in live theater. Each line came out the same way in each performance, and that habit was hard to kick. My teacher and mentor, Nancy Houfek, dared me to show more of myself while I was performing and assigned me a comedic fop from a Restoration comedy. That was the paradigm shift for me. As I analyzed the language, I realized I could unlock the innuendo with context from my life. I didn't have to be afraid that I didn't fit the character perfectly. I had fun revealing the secrets of the words to the audience. I began treating every text like that, even with roles I would never be cast in professionally. Before then, I wasn't connecting myself to my speechwork. I was dutifully fulfilling the correct sounds and strict

INTRODUCTION

structure of the text, with very little fun and no room for change. I was understandable to the audience's minds but not their hearts.

I teach speech because I want to guide actors to find themselves in an author's words the way I found myself in that Restoration comedy. Yes, you may be performing someone else's words. Yes, you may sometimes be performing in an accent that is not your own. But you're still in there. You are a living, breathing person who is going through something when you get up to perform. That's not just fanciful language about acting. The act of standing up in front of people and letting them look at you and listen to you will stir up real sensations. You're having a real experience. When you can connect your own, real experience of living to the structure of the text and its articulation, then you'll elicit a deeper understanding from the audience: empathy. They'll be able to not only hear your words and their meaning but feel them as well.

Before I move on, it's important for me to acknowledge the teachers whose work has inspired what and how I teach. I gained skills and my love of speech from Edith Skinner, Timothy Monich, and Lilene Mansell's *Speak with Distinction* as taught to me by Diego Daniel Pardo. I then studied the art of teaching from one of Skinner's students—my aforementioned mentor, Nancy Houfek, at the American Repertory Theater Institute at Harvard. It was there I met David Hammond and absorbed his methodology around finding the ins and outs of language. From there I studied voice pedagogy under Catherine Fitzmaurice and expanded my understanding of what speech could be with Dudley Knight's great book, *Speaking with Skill*. I shadowed and emulated two fantastic and wildly different teachers, Barbara Adrian and Jeff Morrison, while teaching my first voice and speech classes. I went on to study Knight-Thompson Speechwork with Phil Thompson, Andrea Caban, Erik Singer, and Eliza Simpson and was eventually certified in that methodology. I then had the pleasure of teaching at the Yale School of Drama with Beth McGuire, who profoundly influenced my teaching as we brainstormed to meet the changing needs of the actors. I mention these teachers, not to instill a sense of pedigree or hierarchy, but because without their work I wouldn't have the exercises that I offer you or even teach voice and speech at all. All the books, workshops, and faculty meetings I've consumed live inside me and inside this book. I highly recommend checking out all their work if this book sparks an interest in you.

My most important teachers, however, are my students past and present. My methodology comes directly from their questions and sometimes demands. I prioritized the topics in this book based on their needs and curiosities, which were different from the acting students' needs and curiosities in the time that my teachers were coming up. This book is my attempt to meet the needs of twenty-first-century acting students head-on. There was a time when every actor learned a "heightened" dialect for use in poetry and Shakespeare. Speech class was about sounding a certain way, but we no longer expect 21-year-old actors to leave drama school and be immediately cast in roles where they'd use an accent that sounds halfway between the East Coast of the United States and Buckingham Palace. We have a different awareness of how an actor's identity influences the roles they'll get and how they should sound in those roles. To that end, instead of teaching speech through the lens of what was once called a "standard" accent, I begin with a rich understanding of text and how to analyze it, move into a deep exploration of speech anatomy and how it works, then guide the actors through a deep dive into their own sounds and how they use them. Students leave with a strong awareness of how to use their own speech instruments and, when necessary for a specific role, how to take on new habits.

My guiding principle is that you are what makes you special. The first year of acting training is often spent trying to remove the extra stuff that actors put into their performances because they think that's how the character should behave. I remember even trying to change my clothing style to better fit my "type." I removed myself from the equation. Through good training, actors learn to be in touch with the realities of their own bodies, voices, and emotional lives, so that they can be present with those realities even when they're portraying imaginary circumstances. The same can be true for speech. Yes, actors need to transform, but a destination on a map is useful only if you know where you're starting from. If you ignore the wealth of sounds that you use day in and day out to shape the world and get your needs met, you'll be working without a personal connection to language. Your personal, individual dialect is called your **idiolect**. Using this book, you're going to teach yourself what your idiolect is, and hopefully come to love and respect it. It's how you as a real human person reach out and try to change the world around you one thought at a time.

INTRODUCTION

That brings me to core principle number two: if you don't know why you're opening your mouth to speak a bit of text in performance, then you shouldn't. I use language from Konstantin Stanislavski's system of actor training to describe that "why." He calls it the "objective." What are you trying to get from whomever or whatever you're speaking to? All the different ways you go about meeting that objective are the tactics or actions: I'm getting what I want flirtingly, threateningly, carefully, bragadociously, etc. This can go much further than the "mood" of how you're speaking. The structure of the text is a tactic in itself. Just think about why you would give someone quick, short answers versus an entire speech to answer the same question. The text is on purpose for the character, as are articulation choices. Think about the times you might really hit a final "T" at the end of a though**T**. (Note to the editor: if you can find a way to make the book spit a little bit on my scene partner, the reader, that would be great.) So, if a teacher or director asks for a harder final "T," an actor's first exploration could be how that note gets them what they need from their scene partner.

My final core principle is that speechwork is sensitive territory. A final "T" is an easy thing for me to ask for, but the sounds of a person's speech go much deeper than the muscles of the tongue. A person's dialect is the sum of all the people who were ever important to them, consciously or not. It's *aural identity*. I speak with my mother's nasality, my high school best friend's "TR" sounds, the musicality of New York City's white gay culture (which appropriates sounds from New York City's Black and Latinx/Latine gay culture), and the "TN" sound that the aforementioned Nancy Houfek instilled in me for the pronunciation of "gluten." I took all those sounds directly to my heart and they stuck in my speech as part of my identity. To change them is to toy with the man I've become, and that process can be very sensitive. The study of speech doesn't need to strip you of your identity. Learning about your speech can affirm and reinforce what makes you unique and marketable.

On top of personal sensitivity, differences in the way that certain communities of people speak English have historically been used as a tool of oppression. Racism, classism, sexism, heterosexism, ableism, ageism, nationalism, and all the systemic -isms that I've forgotten here have ever-changing rules about what kinds of speech are acceptable or "professional." Those kinds of judgmental standards have been used against certain communities in order to put them down or keep them from gaining status. It is beyond time that we are cognizant of that fact in speech training for actors, so that teachers aren't playing out oppressive tropes in the classroom. It is not in the scope of this introductory book for me to teach directors and teachers that speech notes should have more thought-out, respectful reasons than "It sounds better." I firmly believe that intelligibility doesn't begin with the upper middle class, educated, white, able-bodied, heterosexual accent that has traditionally been taught to actors as "neutral." (Or else nobody would ever understand plays or movies performed in accents—and I'm a dialect coach; that would be the end of my career.) I believe intelligibility truly begins with analysis of the structure of the language. When *you* make *the* wrong words *of a* thought important, it's more difficult *to* understand. I will also say that changing your accent will eventually be a necessary, useful, and hopefully fun part of your acting career. Practicing how to change your sounds is also a great way to get to know your instrument. There's a right way and a wrong way to do it, however, and the right way begins with discarding notions of good sounds and bad sounds—of pretty accents and ugly accents. So, in this book, we're going to practice removing judgment from how we listen to speech sounds. We'll start with respectfully, lovingly discussing the accent that is often the hardest to listen to but closest to your identity: your own.

Assumptions and -isms

I've laid out this book to build a respectful relationship to your speech, but I have to work under a few assumptions in order to accomplish that. The first assumption is a touch ableist in that I assume that you can speak. Not all actors can, and it will do us good as artists and humans to remember that. If you have a speech or communication disorder, this book can still be useful to you. I'm not a speech pathologist, so this book cannot cure any speech or communication disorders, but it can help you learn about whatever speech you use and how to employ it mindfully as an actor-artist.

My second assumption is that you're acting with English-language text. Many of the explorations this book will take you through could be applied to other languages, but most are focused on English grammar and sounds. I have, however, attempted to make this book applicable

INTRODUCTION

to every dialect of English by instructing you to analyze and describe the sounds you actually make rather than teaching you specific sounds. Because of that, this book can be a valuable resource to someone whose first language is not English, so long as they're exploring their English speech.

Assumption three is that you're either working in a Western, probably Stanislavski-based acting tradition, like the one you'll explore in the other titles in this series, or interested in learning about it. There are so many fabulous ways to be an actor around the world, but I'm honestly not versed in all of them. I conceptualize acting through a US-American and Russian lens, so that's the acting language I will refer to, like the specific use of the term "objective." I'm optimistic that the skills in this book can be applied to other theatrical styles, but I will allow you, dear reader, to lead that experimentation and report back. I would truly love to hear about your performance style and how the study of your own idiolect intersects with it.

My last assumption is that you have access to some kind of recording device and a way to store and play back those recordings. The main recording is coming up right after the introduction, so if you need to borrow a device, now's the time. The rest of the exercises where I ask you to use a recording device were actually designed to be done with a partner or a small group, but I have adapted them for solo work by incorporating a recording device. Instead of listening to a recording of yourself, you and a partner can talk about what you felt and heard. You'll also eventually need a pack of colored pencils for an exercise I designed for a pack of twenty-four colors.

How to use this book

I've reversed the order of the material in this book from the way I was taught speech. I was taught how to warm up, how to perform each speech sound in a specific way, and how to make sense of language last. That gave me almost a year of speech training in my second year of drama school before I learned how to approach the lines that I started working with on my very first day. We'll start this book with the skills needed to analyze and make choices about your text, so that you can apply those skills immediately. From there, we'll jump to anatomy, musicality, and then the sounds of your accent. You can follow the order as I've laid it out, or you can jump around. The aspects of speech that we'll explore in each chapter all affect one another, so there's no perfect spot to begin. You may find yourself yearning to reread a section once you've had a lightbulb moment in another section. Feel free to follow your curiosity.

I use three different kinds of activities in this book: *play*, *exercise*, and *idiolectsploration*. In the *play* category, I want you to try out a new concept and explore how far you can go with it. Speech habits form for efficiency's sake. If we had to think specifically about how we speak all the time, we wouldn't have any brain space left to think our thoughts. Speech habits make it so that we move in a similar way all the time, so we can forget about how we speak, and eventually we lose most of the sensations of speaking. A playful exploration of possibilities with no goal in mind will allow you to bring some of your attention back onto your speech as you expand the possibilities of movement beyond your habits. It might lead you to funny noises or a speech sound that you recognize. Who knows? The world's our oyster. An *exercise* has more of a goal in mind. For example, I might ask you to practice pronouncing three different kinds of "T" sounds. Exercises are skill building and will help you find flexibility and awareness of your speech mechanisms. Since they tend to be more specific, I've created companion videos to help you with some of the exercises. A list of videos is included in Appendix D. Last, we have the *idiolectsplorations*. You'll take the awareness that you've built from play, mix it with some of the skills you learned in the exercises, and then explore your own accent—your own way of using sounds to change the world around you. At the end of the book, you'll have a collection of idiolectsplorations that will amount to a detailed study of your idiolect.

The International Phonetic Alphabet

When we start analyzing speech sounds, I'll reference the **International Phonetic Alphabet**, or IPA for short. The IPA is a group of symbols used to write down speech sounds. It's part of why I fell in love with speech class. I was really good at using the IPA. Many of my classmates were not, so they didn't love speech class like I did. As a teacher,

I loved the IPA because it was less stressful for me to grade than a performance, which is fairly subjective. It's a real shame that I spent our time like that, because the IPA isn't the point of speech class—speech is. If the symbols of the IPA are daunting or if you're one of the many humans with a reading disorder and the IPA is a barrier, just scrap it and describe your speech with words. /t̚/ is just shorthand for a "T" that doesn't explode. I'd be more excited to know that you had the awareness of the fact that your "T" didn't explode than I would be to know that you got the symbol right. I'm more interested in helping you find physical awareness and speech skills rather than the written tool to describe sounds. Again, follow your curiosity.

Accent, dialect, and idiolect

I'm already using and abusing a few terms that we should take a peek at. The first is **language**—the way we use words in different formations called **grammar** to communicate. Under the umbrella of "language," we also have **accent**, which is the way a spoken language is pronounced. Some languages, like English, have different pronunciations in different communities, so those languages have multiple accents. We also have a separate term, **dialect**, which is a form of a language that differs from another form of the same language because of accent and at least one other quality, such as vocabulary or grammar.[1] I speak with a US midwestern dialect, so I use the word "sweater" and you can hear a quality of "R" at the end of that word. Someone speaking in a London dialect would call that same article of clothing a "jumper," and the end of that word would not have a quality of "R" in the pronunciation. Speakers of each dialect will mostly be able to understand one another, but there are differences. Some in the US theater scene use the term "dialect" to describe a form of English that people would have as their native language and reserve "accent" for the sounds of English as a second language. I try to stick with what the linguists have to say on the subject. Last, and most important, we

---

[1] Behrens and Parker, *Language in the Real World*.

have the term "idiolect," which I've already defined—and which you'll define throughout—as a person's own, unique dialect.

This work is about you—who you are, where you come from, and how you bring your fullest sense of self to the text you work on. I'm excited that you're here and humbled to get to explore your speech with you. And on that note ... (Editor: the drumroll goes here.)

1
A SNAPSHOT OF YOU

The first step to understanding your idiolect is to hear it and get to know it. What's fun about the way we speak is that it's always changing. We're constantly adapting as we join new communities or lose touch with old ones. In order to truly study your speech as it is right now, we need to freeze it in time. You're going to record yourself so you can analyze your speech over the course of this book. If that makes you squirm, remember: the way you speak is connected to everyone you've ever loved. It's their gift to you. It's good to practice listening to yourself without judgment. I know, easier said than done, but don't let your inner critic stop you from transforming your speech from something you take for granted into a mindful, empowered choice you can make as an artist. You have a great accent. Let's learn about it!

For this section, you should record yourself speaking to a partner. If you're working through this book on your own, call someone on the telephone or on videoconferencing technology. This should take a bit less than fifteen minutes total.

Storytelling and conversation

The best way to hear what your speech sounds like is to speak from the heart. In this section, you're going to speak naturally, without a script or a plan, so you have a record of what you sound like during everyday conversation.

Start recording. Take one or two minutes to tell a story from your childhood, and then record one or two minutes of the ensuing conversation, if there is one. Here are some prompts if you're finding it difficult to think of something to talk about.

- What is the worst trouble you ever got into as a kid?
- Describe the biggest family celebration you can remember.
- What is the most vivid dream you can remember?

Reading

Sometimes, we sound differently when we read or perform memorized text. Let's get a snapshot of what you sound like when someone else chooses your words! Record yourself reading the following, adapted from *Stella Starchild*, by Ricardo Pérez González [*Stella Starchild* is copyright 2020 by Ricardo Pérez González].

Stella Starchild, daughter of the Sun and Moon, couldn't sleep. It was a sunny midnight afternoon (see back then there was no difference between night and day) and Stella's parents were at it again. "How are the Children of the Earth to live? You burn much too hotly for them to survive," argued the Moon. "Harrumph! If it were up to you, they'd trip and break their necks in the dark, you shine so weakly!" accused the Sun. And the heavenly realm was ringing with their fulgent fury as the two went back and forth, back and forth, not budging about the finer points of illumination. For all their supposed concern for the Children of the Earth's health, they never grasped the fact that those very same Children were suffering thanks to their dazzling disagreement. But Stella Starchild, daughter of the Sun and Moon, noticed. She observed as sure enough, the bellowing heat of the Sun made it hard for the Children of the Earth to live as it scorched their crops to smoking ash and brought thirst to their throats. And she watched as the Moon reflected the light of the Sun (for that is how the Moon glows) into the Children's eyes, obscuring their vision and confusing their path as they stumbled through the day-night. All the while the two squabbled in the blue sky above and failed to take notice of those around them, not the Children of the Earth, not their own daughter, Stella. Stella knew something had to be done, but what? "There's only one thing for it," thought Stella, resolved to help. "When my parents share the sky, their mythic discord erupts in the heavens and showers upon the earth. They'll have to be separated, or else." And so, Stella Starchild sprang straight into the middle of her parents' quarrel and exclaimed "halt!" So surprised were they by the interruption they stopped their mouths and listened as Stella described her big plan. "You can no longer share the sky," Stella proclaimed. "How am I to shine aloft without your Obi's radiance!?" balked the Moon. "Yes! And how am I to know I exist without your Zaza's reflection!?" bemoaned the Sun. "You will always be just beyond the horizon from one another, waiting to trade places," their daughter replied. "With time and distance, you will learn to support one another the way you used to, when your love and warmth created me." The Sun and the Moon admired the pure wisdom of their child. A huge tear welled up in the Sun's eye and evaporated into wisps of steam. "And you, Stella? Where will you be?" they asked. Stella flinched, sniffled, then finally shrugged. "By myself?" She hadn't thought that far ahead. She was stumped. "I'll tell you, Stella," said the Moon. "You will be with us, always. We will clear a space of honor for you in the northern skies, and your splendid brilliance will be a guide and teacher to all the Children of the Earth, as you have been a guide to us." And that is how Stella Starchild, daughter of the Sun and the Moon, the first child of divorce, became the North Star.

Playing with sentence structures

We'll do a deep dive into grammar soon, but for this section, just know that we structure the language we use in different ways depending on what we're using the language for. Let's get a sample of how you communicate a few different structures! For each of the following structures, record yourself reading the sentence and then make up a sentence using the same structure.

1 Declaration: Joy had eight slices of pizza last night.
2 Yes or no question: Do you want chicken for dinner?
3 Open question: What is your favorite word?
4 Command: Sit anywhere you'd like.
5 Negative command: Don't lose your purse.
6 If/then statement: If we go out tonight, then we should stay in tomorrow.

14 INTRODUCTION TO SPEECHWORK FOR ACTORS

7   List of three or more items: I want to buy a shirt, slacks, and a belt for the party.
8   Multiple subjects: Mandy and Patti have been working for hours.
9   Multiple verbs: I ate shellfish and had an allergic reaction.
10 Independent clauses: I finished cleaning and Jack practiced the ukulele.
11 Dependent clause: When I was an actor, I hated tap dancing.
12 Contrast: I live in a red house, but you live in a blue house.
13 Parenthetical: Alistair and Gordon (the Rappaport twins) were late to the match.
14 Renaming: I had the best food ever: passionfruit.

Word lists

Last, we have some pronunciation we should listen to. Record yourself reading the following words. If you pronounce a word in multiple ways, record all your pronunciations. Linguists use closely related words, or **minimal pairs**, to compare accents and dialects. This is your "accent tag," like the YouTube trend of the same name.

1. fleece	2. fleas	3. happy	4. happiness	5. between	6. rated
7. irrational	8. fussing	9. pin	10. pen	11. pit	12. pet
13. pat	14. path	15. pan	16. spank	17. but	18. about
19. tuba	20. tuber	21. word	22. burn	23. bird	24. berth
25. burst	26. cartoon	27. tune	28. root	29. rude	30. rook
31. rut	32. obey	33. Olympics	34. court	35. caught	36. claw
37. cloth	38. clot	39. calm	40. father	41. farther	42. face
43. phase	44. price	45. prize	46. joist	47. joys	48. pouch
49. plows	50. sear	51. sears	52. seer	53. hare	54. hairy
55. hairs	56. poor	57. pure	58. fork	59. form	60. force
61. ford	62. foreign	63. cha-chas	64. char	65. ire	66. buyer
67. hour	68. flower	69. curl	70. coil	71. curry	72. merry
73. marry	74. Mary	75. old	76. ultra	77. sing	78. singing

Idiolectsploration: Responding to the sample

Welcome to your first idiolectsploration! These exercises are where you'll really learn about what makes your idiolect special! Now that you're done recording, have a listen. Email this recording to yourself or put it in a cloud for safekeeping and write your future self an email with your observations. What is your general reaction to hearing your speech? Do you recognize anything in your speech that is similar to the speech of other people in your life? Do you sound like people from any of the places you've lived? Does anything stand out?

Idiolectsploration: Social location

You have now documented your very own native accent—your idiolect. Your idiolect is the aural history of your life. You've been gleaning your idiolect from all the communities that have been important to you since just before you were born. Use Table 1 to brainstorm the following details about your life and think about the ways they may have influenced your speech.

The middle of the Venn diagram that includes your family, friends, socioeconomic background, sex, gender, race, ethnicity, sexuality, education level, and all the places you've ever lived is called your **social location**. These are the people, places, and things that have influenced who you are, how you see the world, what privileges you may or may not enjoy, and what your speech sounds like. We'll get back to this recording anon, but for now enjoy it for what it is—the sound of your life story.

TABLE 1 *Social Location*

Place(s) of origin / first language	Age / Date of birth

Sex / Gender / Sexuality	Race / Ethnicity

Socioeconomic background / Education	Places you've lived

Miscellaneous pertinent information

2
MEET YOUR TEXT

I once asked my acting faculty colleague, Gregory Wallace, which speech skills would be the most beneficial to first-year actors in the first weeks of the semester. His response was that they always needed a more specific understanding of language. Relatively new actors don't necessarily know what they are saying when they approach new text, so they emphasize the wrong things and lose the meaning. Sometimes, even worse, they may know that they don't understand the lines, wing it anyway, and hope if they sound emotional while saying the words in order, the audience will glue the pieces together. I played Romeo in tenth grade, way before my first acting class, so I understand that impulse so well. I threw the cart way before the horse and tried to "reveal" something with text that I could barely memorize because I had no idea what I was saying. What I know now, and what Gregory emphasized, is that even for more modern or straightforward texts, a deep dive into the language structure is a necessary first step. You, dear reader, might already be working on a scene or a monologue, so I made sure that this chapter came early. If you can solidify your understanding of what your character is saying—really get into it—then you can begin to make discoveries about why you're saying it. The result will be a more specific use of language in your monologue or scene work to go after what your character needs.

The following is my way of organizing text, which is a mash-up of skills I learned from Shakespearean scholar, David Hammond's course "Talking Shakespeare" at the American Repertory Theater Institute, Catherine Fitzmaurice's "telegramming" exercises, and a deep-dive exploration of English grammar. In this way of working, I mark my text with pencil so that I can see what's important in the language and how those important bits are being arranged. By marking the text in this way, I begin to see patterns jump out and make themselves clear.

Some useful grammar concepts before we begin

I had plenty of experience speaking and even writing essays by the time I got to drama school, but I couldn't quickly tell you the difference between a clause and a phrase. They are important tools playwrights use to shape a character's language, however, so it's important to know what to do with them when you're speaking words that aren't your own. Here's a crash course in the grammar that we'll be looking for in this chapter. Go slowly and read this section twice. It really puts the "crash" into "crash course." Now, heads up, some of the jargon below is going to sound like "rules," and not every English speaker is going to follow these "rules," so not all characters will either. Language is always changing, and certain dialects of English will have slightly different grammatical structures than others. No dialect is better than another, and differences in a character's grammar make for great character development if you spend the time to learn about what makes that grammar specific.

We'll start with the **parts of speech**, or word categories, that we'll be spending the most time with. I call the categories of words that we can close our eyes and imagine, remember, smell, or do the **images** of the text. These are the bulk of the sentence—the words we can have a relationship with. The parts of speech that I lump together as images are the verbs, nouns, adjectives, and adverbs. We'll do a deep dive shortly, but all these terms are defined by their relationship to the other terms. So, to start, the **verb** is the word or words in the sentence that communicate what the subject does. A **noun** is a person, place, thing, concept, etc., that can either perform the action of a verb or have the action of the verb done to it. An **adjective** is a word that modifies a noun, and an **adverb** is a word that modifies a verb. Let's jump in!

Verbs

Again, the verb is the word or words in the sentence that communicate what the subject does. We'll get to the subject in a bit. The verb can be one word, such as "runs," or multiple words, such as "have been running." When multiple words work together to build a single part of speech, they are called a **phrase**. So multiple words that work together to form a verb are called a **verb phrase**, for example, "Ron *has been running*." **Conjugation** is when a verb changes its spelling and pronunciation to communicate:

1. **Person**—the verb can match the point of view of the noun it belongs to, e.g., "I *am*." "You *are*."
2. **Number**—the verb can match the number of its noun, e.g., "He *is*." "They *are*."
3. **Tense**—tense communicates when the verb takes place, e.g., "She *runs*." "She *ran*."
4. **Aspect**—aspect signals the degree of completeness of the verb, e.g., "She *is running*." "She *had run*." "He *done run*." "She *be singing*."
5. **Mood**—a mood is the way a sentence is being used.
    a. **Indicative mood**—communicates a fact as a declaration or question, e.g., "She ran." "Did she run?"
    b. **Subjunctive mood**—communicates something hypothetical, wishful, doubtful, or just not factual, e.g., "She wishes she were running." "If she got up earlier, then she would run."
    c. **Imperative mood**—communicates a command, e.g., "Run!" In the imperative mood, the subject is not always in the sentence because the listener is being commanded. In the example "Run!" the subject is a tacit "you."[1]

A **participle** is the "-ing" form of a verb commonly used in conjugation to express tense, aspect, or mood, e.g., "I had been *running*." A participle will always have **auxiliary verbs**, or helping verbs, when it is part of a verb conjugation. In the last example, "had been," are the auxiliary verbs that let us know the tense and aspect of "running."

When an "-ing" verb doesn't have an auxiliary verb attached to it, something non-verb is happening! A **participial phrase** is a group of words that begin with a participle, have no auxiliary verbs, and act as adjectives or adverbs. "*Walking home*, I found a wallet." We know that

---

[1]Nordquist, "Definition and Examples of Major and Minor Moods in English Grammar."

"I" is the subject, and "I walking home" doesn't make sense, so "walking" isn't the verb. This "-ing" form of the verb "to walk" is a participle, and "walking home" is a participial phrase. That means "walking home" is acting as an adverb modifying "found."

"*Running* is my favorite activity." In this example, "running" is a **gerund**, an "-ing" form of a verb that is used as a noun, in either the subject or the object of the thought. **Infinitive verbs** are verbish words in the present tense with "to" in front of them. Similar to gerunds, infinitives can be used as nouns, e.g., "*To eat* was my only wish." Infinitives can also be used as adjectives, e.g., "This is my favorite thing *to eat*," or adverbs, e.g., "I want *to eat*."

Nouns

A noun is a person, place, thing, concept, etc., that can either do a verb or be done to. Nouns can be single words, such as "Ron," "hope," or "Vienna," or **noun phrases**, such as "my kitten," "the tower guards," or "the blue house at the end of the cul-de-sac in the town where I grew up."

The **subject** is the noun that does the action of the verb. "*Ron* writes." "*She* is speaking to Mishy." I don't love the term. "Subject" is not the same thing as "subject matter." The subject is often not the point of the thought, or even the most important noun. It's just the noun that does the verb. "He wrote a letter to the king about our foes." In this sentence, "a letter," "the king," and "our foes" are all nouns, but our verb is "wrote" and the only word that "wrote" is "he."

An **object** is a noun built into the verb phrase that receives the action of the verb. The **direct object** answers the question "Verbed what?" An **indirect object** always has a direct object nearby and answers the question "To or for whom?" In the example "Ron baked a cake for Ricardo," Ron baked what? A cake. "A cake" is the direct object. Ron baked a cake to or for whom? Ricardo. Ricardo is the indirect object. (Fun to note: the difference between "who" and "whom" is that "whom" is the object form.) "Ricardo" would still be the indirect object if we rearranged the words to say "Ron baked Ricardo a cake." The answers to the questions "Verbed what?" and "Verbed to or for whom?" remain the same. Just because "Ricardo" follows the verb, that doesn't mean we have a murder on our hands or a cake named Ricardo.

Adjectives

An adjective is a **modifier**, or a word that specifies the meaning of another word—for nouns specifically. Adjectives modify nouns by answering the questions, "Which noun?" "What kind of noun?" or "How many nouns?" In the example "I love the blue house," we may ask "Which house?" The *blue* house. "Blue" is the adjective. "The marbles that fell on the floor are a choking hazard." What kind of marbles? The marbles *that fell on the floor*. "That fell on the floor" is the adjective. Since it is made up of multiple words, it is called the **adjectival phrase**.

Adverbs

An adverb is a word or phrase that modifies a verb. Adverbs answer the questions "Why?" "How?" "When?" or "Where?" For the sentence "I ran quickly," I would ask, "How did I run?" Quickly. We will also see **adverbial phrases**, like in the example "I ran to the grocery store." We could ask, "Where did I run?" To the grocery store. "To the grocery store" is an adverbial phrase that modifies the verb "run." If we think back to our participial phrase, "walking home" in the sentence, "*Walking home*, I found a wallet," we can see that it answers the question, "How?" or, "When?" and not, "Which?" or "What kind?" That means it's acting as an adverb.

Analyzing the text

We don't think about grammar when we're speaking. We hold the images of language somewhere inside us. When we choose to speak, we offer the images inside us one by one to make a point. The order that we present the images in is important—it provides structure. Different structures mean different things. We make peaks and valleys to convey to the listener what's important about the structures we're using. *Language moves.* You may have already heard the term "**operative word**" in class or rehearsal. This is one way to describe moving to a peak when an image is important to the point of a sentence. Operative words shouldn't be considered in isolation though, because the movement of language isn't just about bouncing from peak to peak;

it's about the entire journey. It's about how one peak rolls into another and then falls away like the waves in a turbulent ocean. In the following section, we're going to explore my favorite way of meeting a piece of text where it is—to uncover what kind of movement is possible—so that we can imbue the language with meaning and context. We'll use one of my favorite poems, "The New Colossus," by Emma Lazarus, which was written about, and then displayed in, the Statue of Liberty.

Thoughts

Let's begin by finding the distinct thoughts. In life, you have a need that you want met—the impulse to speak—so you breathe and speak without knowing exactly which words you'll use to make your point. There might (on occasion) be a few twists and turns in your thought, but it remains one impulse and comes to a feeling of completeness. Maybe then you get a new impulse for another thought, or you may give your partner a turn to speak. Next you … Sometimes you may even interrupt one thought to start a new one (see what I did there?). A playwright's job is to plan the thoughts that each character uses. It's the actor's job to make them seem as unplanned as if you thought of them on the spot when you needed them. Step 1 on that journey is to know where each thought starts and stops.

Most thoughts you'll encounter will be complete sentences, so let's start there. The criterion for a complete sentence is that there is **subject-verb agreement**, or a verb that is conjugated in accordance with the subject of the sentence. "I run" and "She runs" both have a subject and a verb that is conjugated to match that subject. "Runs" is not a complete sentence because there's no subject. When we're commanding someone in the imperative mood, the subject is a tacit (assumed and not present) "you." For example, in the command "Go!" it is understood that I'm talking to "you," so "Go!" is a complete sentence.

Let's find the first thought of "The New Colossus" (p. 33). I like to start by looking for the verb. The first line doesn't have anything verb-like, so that's not a complete thought. In the second line we have "conquering," but it ends in "-ing," so it's not a stand-alone verb like "runs." There's no auxiliary verb here, so we're looking at a participial phrase. In this case, "conquering" is describing what kind of limbs the brazen giant has, so it's acting as an adjective. That means we don't have a verb yet, so let's keep going! In line three we have "shall stand." That's an auxiliary verb and a verb! The line also starts with "here," which tells us where something is happening! So, in a different word order, this line could say, "shall stand here at our sea-washed, sunset gates." I think we've found our verb, but let's keep going to check. There's nothing verbish in line four, but line five starts with "is." That "is" connects "flame" and "the imprisoned lighting." If we zoom out further, we have "whose flame is the imprisoned lightning." Something doesn't feel complete about that. The word "whose" is a clue that this phrase is acting as an adjective describing "the mighty woman with a torch" and not acting like a verb. Then in line six we have a period and the sentence is done. That means "shall stand" is indeed part of our verb phrase. Now we need a subject, so we need to find out who or what is doing the standing. The one doing the standing is "a mighty woman with a torch," or, more simply, "woman." Everything else in lines one through five is modifying "a woman shall stand." That means everything from the first line to "Mother of Exiles" in line six is our first thought.

    Let's backtrack for a minute. "Whose flame is the imprisoned lightning" has a subject, "flame," and a verb, "is." How is that not a thought? Well, unfortunately, not every instance of subject-verb agreement will automatically be a whole thought. A **clause** is a phrase in a larger sentence that has subject-verb agreement. An **independent clause** can stand on its own and still make sense, like in the sentence "*I ran to the store* and *I bought potatoes*." In that thought, "I ran to the store" and "I bought potatoes" are both independent clauses connected into one thought by the conjunction "and." A **dependent clause**, on the other hand, is a phrase that is one part of a larger sentence and includes subject-verb agreement but that cannot stand on its own. Take the thought "*When I went to Houston*, I ate so much queso." In this example, "When I went to Houston" leaves you hanging, even though the verb "went" has agreement with the subject "I." That hanging feeling means this phrase is a dependent clause—it's dependent on the rest of the sentence to make sense. The word "when" is the clue. It means that the clause is modifying something. In this case it's specifying when "I ate." Back to the poem, the word "whose" is our clue that we have a dependent clause.

Again, not every character is going to speak in complete sentences. When I'm looking for the thoughts in a piece of text, I also include interrupted thoughts—whether the speaker interrupts themself or is interrupted by someone or something else. I also include **interjections**—the exclamations and outbursts that lack subject-verb agreement—if they're not connected to a larger thought. Examples include Polonius's exclamation in Shakespeare's *Hamlet*, "*O!* I am slain," or in *Cymbeline*, Imogen's longer, "*O! For a horse with wings!*" Exclamations are fun because they can communicate something quick and specific or act as a springboard that catapults you into the following thought. "Fie!" "Crikey!" "Dang!" They are loaded words and super-useful bits of text.

Exercise: Marking thoughts

"The New Colossus" by Emma Lazarus is included on page 33. Read it and use braces {} to mark where each thought starts and stops. For example, {"Keep, ancient lands, your storied pomp!" cries she / With silent lips.}

Play: Speaking thoughts

Sit in a chair and read the text. When the first thought ends, stand up; when the next ends, sit down; and so on. If standing and sitting quickly isn't your style, then you can turn your head, point your finger, or move your eyes to two different objects in the room. Play with this blocking as if it were a newfangled directing style. What are you learning about the text? What's your body doing?

Function words

Important words create bulk thought. Write images alone text almost understandable. Sorry about that. I just wrote "The important words create the bulk of the thought. If I write in images alone, the text is almost understandable." The words that I left out of my esoteric sentences are called **function words**. They are the nonimages. We can't close our eyes and have a vision or sensation of them beyond how they look on a page or sound when we say them. They are the words that organize our images and let us know how we're using them. Unless function words are specifically being pointed out in juxtaposition to one another, they are not the important words of a thought. Some function words become so unimportant that their pronunciations change. These pronunciations are called **weak forms**, and they are a necessary component of the movement of each thought. They're the valleys, and without the valleys, there can be no peaks! As we've already seen with "when" and "whose," function words can also be clues about what structures we're using and how we're presenting the images to make our point. There's so much to be gained by a deep dive into the function words! Grab your snorkel, because we're going in!

Exercise: Marking function words

The following is a list of the types of function words with hints about how they might be used in a thought. Read "The New Colossus" by Emma Lazarus and find each type of function word. Figure out exactly how it's functioning and then cross it out. It may seem silly now to spend the time to analyze the difference between "a cow" and "the cow," but when all is completed and you begin the acting task, you'll be working from a place of deep and subtle understanding. If you're not sure about a word, look it up in a dictionary. Some words will be function words in some contexts and image words in other contexts.

1. **Articles**—words that introduce a noun (a, an, the).
   a. The **definite article**, "the," points to a specific individual noun.
   b. The **indefinite articles**, "a, an," point to nonspecific members of that noun group.
   c. Think about the contextual difference between "the queen" and "a queen."
   d. Find all the articles, locate the nouns they belong to, take a moment to think about the context, and cross them out.
   e. The first article in "The New Colossus" is "the." We're talking about a specific "brazen giant," not just any old one.
2. **Conjunctions**—words that connect images or whole clauses in a thought (and, but, if, or, nor, because, while, whereas, etc.). Conjunctions are great because they can glue images or

clauses together to make multiple subjects, objects, or verb phrases in the same thought. They are like the directions for the road of the text. "And" can mean that you're taking a turn toward building. "Or" is a turn toward choosing. "But" can be a turn toward doubting.

    a Find all the articles, think about how they're affecting the journey of the thought, and cross them out. It's not the function word that's important; it's how the turn affects the images.

    b Our first thought has the conjunction "and," which connects "her name Mother of Exiles" to the dependent clause "whose flame is the imprisoned lightning." This "and" is a turn in the road toward building our definition of "woman."

3 **Prepositions**—words that show the relationship between images, often spatial (to, from, of, in, on, at, with, etc.).

    a Prepositions are clues that we have a phrase.
Prepositional phrases act as either adjectives or adverbs.

    b When you see a preposition, figure out what the prepositional phrase is, and then cross the preposition out.

    c We have a preposition in the first line: "brazen giant *of* Greek fame." The preposition "of" can show a relationship of belonging. So this brazen giant is the one that belongs to Greek fame is or related to Greek fame.

    d There's another preposition in that first line: "like." That means "like the brazen giant of Greek fame ..." is all a prepositional phrase, so it's acting as an adjective or adverb. What is it modifying? I think this is modifying the verb "shall stand" because it answers the question "How?" How shall our mighty woman stand? She shall stand "not like the brazen giant of Greek fame, with conquering limbs astride from land to land."

4 **Pronouns**—words that take the place of previously introduced noun(s). Pronouns change their form depending on where they land in the thought:

MEET YOUR TEXT

a Subject (I, you, we, they, she, ze, he, this, that, etc.).

b Object (me, you, us, them, her, zir, him).

c Reflexive (myself, yourself, ourselves, themself, themselves, herself, zirself, himself).

    i Reflexive pronouns are used when the object of the verb is the same as the subject, e.g., "Ron kicked himself."

    ii Interestingly, there is a linguistic trend in the United States in which folks are using reflexive pronouns in the object as a marker of formality instead of referring back to the subject. "If you have any questions, you can ask Darryl or myself," as opposed to "you can ask Darryl or me."

d Possessive (mine, your, our, their, his, zirs, her, hers).

e Find the pronouns. Make sure you know what specific noun each pronoun is referring to and then cross it out. Just like in life, it's important to connect the pronoun with whom or what it's standing in for.

f In our first thought, "whose" is a pronoun! Here, it's showing that the flame belongs to the mighty woman. I think it's really cool that "whose" is the pronoun used here, because it insinuates belonging to a person or maybe an animal and not something inanimate. That means either the flame is hers or we're personifying her torch. One could argue either, but I think since we have "and her name Mother of Exiles" later, we're always talking about her. The imprisoned lightning is her flame. How cool.

g *Pause!* I mentioned quickly that there are situations in which sometimes function words will be peaks in the movement of the thought. Pronouns are often such exceptions. "I love nobody but you." The "you" in this case is the peak of the thought. It's the reason we use a conjunction to turn away from "I love nobody." We don't necessarily have such an exception in "The New Colossus," but I would hear arguments about one or two.

5   **Auxiliary verbs**—"helping" verbs that are added to a verb phrase to change things like tense, active or passive voice, obligations, and conditions (to be, do, have, can, may, might, must, shall, will, should, would, could, ought to, used to, dare, need to). Auxiliary verbs are capable of communicating complex hypotheticals in the past or future, so they may take some extra study to be sure you understand the twists and turns. "By the time you get here, the turkey *will have been being* eaten for an hour." "Will have been being" is all auxiliary to the head verb "eaten," and it is expressing a hypothetical future where a turkey is still in a long, continuous process of being consumed when another event is completed.

   a   Cross out the auxiliary verbs. None of them is an image. They are there in support of the image. Figure out how the auxiliary verb is specifying the head verb.

   b   Be alert! A few auxiliary verbs can be stand-alone (to be, to have, to dare, to need, to do). Make sure they're helping another verb.

   c   "Shall" is our first auxiliary verb. It describes the future tense, but contextually it can hold determination or something like a promise about the future.

6   **Verbs of being**—all the conjugations of "to be" (am, are, is, was, were, will, been, etc.). These words are so unimportant that we often contract them with the subject, like when we turn "I am" into "I'm," or "she is" into "she's." They're known as **copulative verbs**, which direct an adjective back onto the subject.

   a   Find each verb of being. Take a moment to note which adjective is being brought back to the subject and then cross the verb of being out.

   b   Our first thought includes "is." It brings "the imprisoned lightning" back onto "flame." (Remember, this is a dependent clause, so "flame" is a subject and "is" is the verb that agrees with it. You're doing great!)

MEET YOUR TEXT

7 **Negatives**—words that negate an image (not, no). This is a sticky one, because it feels so good to stomp our foot and say, "You're *not* telling the truth." That's a correct response to someone who has just said, "I'm telling the truth," because the "not" is the point. If someone said, "I had noodles," however, and you know they had a sandwich, the "not" isn't the point—"telling the truth" is. Remember: it's the *image* that we have a relationship to and not the *negation*. So, in the previous example, it may actually be a juicier tactic to ride the wave all the way to "truth" instead of spiking the "not." Negation words are so unimportant that they're what get clipped in negative contractions like "didn't, wasn't, don't, won't, shan't, couldn't, and mayn't." Cross the negatives out, but make sure you know what exactly they are negating.

Play: Letting go of the function words

1 Read the text aloud all the way through once.
2 Read the text aloud again, but leave out all the words that are crossed out.
3 Cross out any you missed.
4 Read the text a third time. Leave out the function words, but try to make sense of the language anyway—as if these are the lines that your character speaks to meet their needs.
5 Read the text one last time including the function words, but let them remain unimportant.

Exercise: Organizing the images

Now that you've analyzed and crossed out the words that organize the images, the function words, you can really begin to see the images taking shape in the words that remain. You may have already felt these images come into focus as you let go of the function words. Let's go one step further and find the boundaries of each image so the picture you're creating becomes sharper and sharper.

1 Nouns—On a separate sheet of paper, make a list of all the nouns and noun phrases with all the function words crossed out. Include the noun and all its modifiers, even the longer prepositional phrases. Sometimes there are noun phrases embedded inside larger noun phrases. Let's look at the example sentence "I want to buy the blue house next to the park." "The blue house next to the park" is all one noun phrase, but inside it we also have "the park," which is a second noun phrase within the larger noun phrase. "The park" is its own thing. I would put both "the blue house next to the park" and "the park" on my list of nouns. I wouldn't just put "the blue house" on the list, because that's missing one of its modifiers. We have a more specific house in mind. Remember that you may have gerunds and infinitives acting as nouns! In the first thought of the poem, we have the noun phrase "the brazen giant of Greek frame, with conquering limbs astride from land to land." Going backward through that we have the nouns "land," "conquering limbs astride from land to land," "Greek fame," and "the brazen giant of Greek frame, with conquering limbs astride from land to land."

a Look up any words you're unsure of, or that you don't use every day. Sometimes there's extra context to be found in the second or third definition.

b Underline the **head** of each noun phrase. This is the single-word noun that all the modifiers are specifying. In the noun phrase "Greek fame," the head is "fame," and "Greek" is what kind of fame we're talking about.

c Subjects and objects—On your list of nouns, mark which ones are the subject of their thought, and which are the object. A few thoughts and reminders:

   i Objects are part of the verb phrase.

   ii In commands (also known as the imperative mood), "you" is the subject and not usually included in the thought. You could put "you" on your list for a command, but make a note that it is unspoken.

MEET YOUR TEXT

    iii Sometimes a modifier is attached to more than one noun. In the sentence "The blue walls and floors were too much," the subject, "The blue walls and floors," includes two nominal phrases, "The blue walls" and "The blue floors." You could write them both out if you want. It'll help you connect them when you speak them out loud. Just don't memorize it wrong!

    iv There might be more than one subject or more than one object in each thought. Look for conjunctions and dependent or independent clauses as clues that there are multiple subjects or objects.

    v While English word order is usually subject, verb, object, the subject of the thought isn't always first. Take the sentence "Into the moonlight the dog ran." In this thought, "the dog" is the subject and "into the moonlight" is an adverbial phrase modifying "ran." We know this because of the subject-verb agreement. "The dog ran" makes sense and not "the moonlight ran."

2 Verbs—Now list all the verb phrases.

  a Our first verb phrase is a doozy! "Stand" is the head. Everything that modifies "stand" is part of the verb phrase. I would list something like, "Shall stand here at our sea-washed sunset gates, not like the brazen giant of Greek fame with conquering limbs astride from land to land." That's quite a specific verb!

  b Underline the head of each verb phrase. This is the single-word verb that the rest of the modifiers are specifying.

  c A few thoughts and reminders:

    i Dependent and independent clauses mean that there is more than one subject and verb agreement in the thought. That's okay! This is either a setup and a spike, an escalation, or a change in direction.

    ii Don't forget that infinitives, gerunds, and participial phrases are not being used as verbs. Beware the "-ing."

    iii Copulative verbs link an adjective onto the subject, like "I *am* hungry" or "You *seem* thirsty." When following the copulative verb, the adjective is called a **subjective complement** and is part of the verb phrase.

    iv An **objective complement** is a word that modifies, names, or renames the direct object of the thought. "This makes me *happy*." In this thought, "me" is the direct object and "happy" is renaming me, so it is the objective complement and part of the verb phrase.

3 Modifiers—Go through your lists and make sure you know what your modifiers specify.

    a If it helps, draw arrows from the modifier to the head. Modifiers that you're looking for include adjectives, adverbs, prepositional phrases (which can act as adjectives or adverbs), some infinitives (the ones acting as adjectives or adverbs but not nouns), subjective complements, objective complements, and participial phrases.

    b Ask yourself if these modifiers are acting as adjectives or adverbs. If it helps, try substituting a known adjective or adverb for the modifier you're trying to understand and see if the thought makes sense. "I ran to the grocery store." My adjective swap would be "I ran blue." My adverb swap would be, "I ran quickly." Judging by which swap made more sense, I would say that "to the grocery store" is an adverb and modifying "ran."

4 Go through the text and make sure all the words that are not crossed out are accounted for. Look up any that are left over and decide where they go! It took me a long time to deal with "and her name Mother of Exiles." I decided that since "and" is connecting it to "whose flame is the imprisoned lightning," it's modifying "woman" in the same way.

That was quite a bit of work. Well done for sticking with it. Go through and read the text again now that you're done. Think back to the first time you read it. What's changed?

"The New Colossus" by Emma Lazarus

Not like the brazen giant of Greek fame,

With conquering limbs astride from land to land;

Here at our sea-washed, sunset gates shall stand

A mighty woman with a torch, whose flame

Is the imprisoned lightning, and her name

Mother of Exiles. From her beacon-hand

Glows world-wide welcome; her mild eyes command

The air-bridged harbor that twin cities frame.

"Keep, ancient lands, your storied pomp!" cries she

With silent lips. "Give me your tired, your poor,

Your huddled masses yearning to breathe free,

The wretched refuse of your teeming shore.

Send these, the homeless, tempest-tost to me,

I lift my lamp beside the golden door!"

3
LANGUAGE OF YOUR BODY

In the previous chapter, you analyzed and organized the language of "The New Colossus." You now have a road map of the structure of the text. You found all the noun and verb phrases. Starting from the head of each phrase, you expanded your understanding of the images by folding in all their modifiers. You have a clearer understanding of what images you're employing when you speak this poem to get your argument across. Your analysis has led you to a better intellectual understanding of the twists and turns of the text.

Think for a moment about the images that you use in your daily life. What do you call sporty shoes? Are they tennis shoes, gym shoes, sneakers, trainers, pumps? Do you call the evening meal tea, supper, dinner, or something else? These are words that you don't have to think up. They just come out when you need them. Besides accent, or how the language sounds, one of the main differences between two dialects of the same language is the **lexicon**, or the vocabulary of that dialect. Writers use lexical variation to specify the world of the characters and the dialects they use. Let's do the same thing for your idiolect.

Lexicon

Use Table 2, Idiolect Lexicon, to organize some of your favorite personal vocabulary words. What images do you share with your communities that someone on the outside would have to analyze if they were playing you? Take some time to brainstorm, and then keep your ears open and be mindful of the unique words and phrases you use.

TABLE 2 *Idiolect Lexicon*

Word	Description / definition
Canny	Pleasant or good (Newcastle, UK)
Jawn	Placeholder word for any noun except men or boys (Philadelphia, USA)
Schmear	Edible spread one might put on something like a bagel (Yiddish loanword to New York)

LANGUAGE OF YOUR BODY

How do the words in Table 2 make you feel? Where do you feel those things? When you speak off-the-cuff, you're not picking and choosing your words from your memory as if it's a catalog. Your relationship to words—to images—lives somewhere in your body. We choose our images based on how they make us feel and how we want that to affect our scene partner. When you're speaking a writer's text, however, the language is starting outside of you. You don't have the lifetime of context behind the images the way you do with the lexicon from your idiolect. So, you get to build a physical relationship to the images from scratch.

Let's go back to your analysis of "The New Colossus." How do you feel about the nouns and verbs? What are they to you? How do you wield them for or against your scene partner? Why are they the correct tool to get what you want? Right now, you may not be feeling very deeply about your list of words. Creating your list was a very intellectual exercise. Let's build some context back into the language of the text by personalizing the analysis. This is a way to take language that started its life outside of you and let it affect you. If it affects you, it affects the character you're giving life to. I've seen this work take text that was spoken mechanically and turn it into impulsive communication. I have also seen this work help non-native speakers deepen their relationship to English text by filling in context that previously existed only in their native language. This is the bridge between the intellectual exercise of understanding the text and the artistic exercise of revealing yourself through it. Let's wake up the movement of your body and start the process of letting it be affected by images.

Packaging your images

1. Read "The New Colossus" out loud.
2. Go to your lists of noun and verb phrases and speak each item out loud. Make a box gesture while you say each phrase as if you're packaging the phrase all together as one thing.

3   Read the poem again while making box gestures around all the noun phrases.

   a   Notice how some boxes are bigger than others.

   b   Notice the boxes within boxes.

4   Read "The New Colossus" again while making box gestures around the verb phrases.

   a   Notice how some boxes are bigger than others.

   b   Notice the boxes inside boxes.

5   Combine the three text exercises.

   a   Stand, sit, or change your eye focus at every thought change.

   b   Let the function words fall away in importance.

   c   Make gesture boxes for all your noun phrases, then repeat for all your verb phrases.

   It's a lot to juggle. Just learn from playing and make it fun.

6   Speak the poem aloud without all the body movements, but let them inform your work.

Now that you're physicalizing the movement of the text, we can move on to letting it affect you more deeply. My colleague Beth McGuire calls this next exercise "word soaking," because you're going to steep in the words and let their meaning diffuse through you like tea through hot water. I love that. Usually, I would incorporate Fitzmaurice Voicework tremors as a kind of full-bodied, active meditation as I let my imagination explore the images while I relinquish control of my breath. If that is part of your practice, feel free to include it. You could also do yoga, go for a jog, color in a coloring book, or simply sit comfortably. The important part is that you allow yourself to breathe and follow your imagination, which lives in your body. The following are some of the prompts I use. Feel free to add any that pop into your mind. It might help to record yourself reading each prompt so that you can just start and stop the recording when you're ready to move on instead of finding your place on the page. With practice, this kind of exploration can become a habit and your imagination will provide the prompts as they come.

Word soaking

Body parts

1. If there is a body part on your list of nouns, commit it to memory with all its modifiers attached.
2. Focus on the head of this noun.
   a. Define it for yourself. Be as specific as possible.
   b. Then be as abstract as possible. What other definitions might this word have? Is it a double entendre?
3. See the head of this noun in your mind's eye as it would be written on the page. Notice if there's anything about the shape of the written word that reminds you of its definition.
4. Silently mouth this noun. What do you learn about this word by the movement?
5. Inhale and imagine that you're moving this word into the body part it describes. What does that feel like? If you don't actually have this body part, breathe into the area where this body part would go on a person who has this body part. Does your lack of this body part bring up any specific sensations, memories, fears, wishes, loves, etc.?
6. Speak this word out loud while trying to vibrate this body part with your voice — whatever that means to you.
7. Are there any sensations, memories, dreams, or fears you associate with this body part?
   a. When something comes up, speak the noun with that in mind.
   b. As if there were someone there to hear you, try to make them see and feel this image with just the word.
8. Now speak this noun with all its modifiers attached. How does that specify this body part for you? Does this change the images coming to mind?
9. Take each modifier one by one.

    a What other nouns could they modify? What would be their opposites?

    b Speak the noun and this modifier with this new understanding.

10 Speak the whole thought that this noun belongs in. If you forget, throw caution to the wind and make it up.

11 Rest and breathe. Let your mind wander around this noun and its modifiers.

12 Take a moment and write down anything new, surprising, or useful.

People

1 If there is a person on your list of nouns, commit that word to memory with all its modifiers attached.

2 Focus on the head of this noun.

    a Define it for yourself. Be as specific as possible.

    b Then be as abstract as possible.

    c If this is another character, explore your character's relationship to this person.

3 See the head of this noun in your mind's eye as it would be written on the page. Notice if there's anything about the shape of the written word that reminds you of its definition.

4 Begin to silently mouth this noun. What do you learn about this word by the movement?

5 Think of a person from your life who would play this role.

6 Where in your body does your relationship with this person live? How does that part of you feel in this moment?

7 Speak this word out loud while trying to vibrate this body part with your voice—whatever that means to you.

8 Are there any sensations, memories, dreams, or fears that you associate with this person?

    a If something comes up, speak the noun with that in mind.

LANGUAGE OF YOUR BODY

    b As if there were someone there to hear you, try to make them see and feel this image with just the word.

9 Fold in all the modifiers attached to this person. How do they specify this person for you? Do they change the images coming to mind?

10 Take each modifier one by one.

    a What other nouns could they modify? What would be their opposites?

    b Speak the noun and this modifier with your new understanding.

11 Say the whole thought that this noun belongs in. If you forget, just make it up.

12 Rest and breathe. Let your mind wander around this person and their modifiers.

13 Take a moment and write down anything new, surprising, or useful.

Other concrete nouns

1 Find a noun on your list that you can see, touch, taste, hear, or go to but that isn't a person or body part. Commit it to memory with all its modifiers attached.

2 Focus on the head of the noun. Define it as specifically as possible, then as abstractly as possible. What else could it mean?

3 See the head of this noun in your mind's eye as it would be written on the page. Notice if there's anything about the shape of the written word that reminds you of its definition.

4 Begin to silently mouth this noun. What do you learn about this word by the movement of your mouth?

5 Where in your body does your relationship with this noun live? If you were to have a sensation of this noun, where in your body would that sensation be?

6 Speak this word out loud while trying to vibrate this body part with your voice.

7 Are there any sensations, memories, dreams, or fears that you associate with this noun?
   a If something comes up, speak the noun with that in mind.
   b As if there were someone there to hear you, try to make them see and feel this image with just the word.
8 What would life be like with too much of this noun?
9 What would life be like with a complete lack of this noun?
10 Fold in the modifiers attached to this noun. How do they specify this noun for you? Do they change the images coming to mind?
11 Take each modifier one by one.
   a What other nouns could they modify? What would be their opposites?
   b Speak the noun and this modifier with this new understanding.
12 Say the whole thought. If you forget, forgive yourself and make it up.
13 Rest and breathe. Let your mind wander around this noun and its modifiers.
14 Take a moment and write down anything new, surprising, or useful.

Abstract nouns

1 Find a noun on your list that you can't see, touch, taste, hear, go to, or do—things like hope, melancholy, philosophy. Sometimes it's the actor's choice whether a word is abstract or concrete. What is it to you? What is it to your character?
2 Commit it to memory with all its modifiers attached.
3 Focus on the head of the noun. Define it as specifically as possible, then as abstractly as possible. What else could it mean?
4 See the head of this abstract noun in your mind's eye as it would be written on the page. Notice if anything about the shape of the written word reminds you of its definition.

5. Begin to silently mouth this noun. What do you learn about this word by the movement?
6. Where in your body does your relationship with this noun live? If you were to have a sensation of this abstract noun, where in your body would that sensation be?
7. If that didn't light anything up for you, is there a person who comes to mind when you think of this abstract noun? Maybe they bring up this abstract noun in you. Where does your relationship with that person live in your body?
8. Speak this word out loud while trying to vibrate this body part with your voice.
9. Are there any sensations, memories, dreams, or fears that you associate with this noun?
    a. If something comes up, speak the noun with that in mind.
    b. As if there were someone there to hear you, try to make them see and feel this image with just the word.
10. What would life be like with too much of this noun?
11. What would life be like with a complete lack of this noun?
12. Fold in the modifiers attached to this noun. How do they specify this noun for you? Do they change the images coming to mind?
13. Take each modifier one by one.
    a. What other nouns could they modify? What would be their opposites?
    b. Speak the noun and this modifier with this new understanding.
14. Say the whole thought. If you forget, laugh at yourself and improvise.
15. Rest and breathe. Let your mind wander around this abstract noun and its modifiers.
16. Take a moment and write down anything new, surprising, or useful.

Verbs

1. Find a verb on your list. Commit it to memory with all its modifiers attached—adverbs, auxiliary verbs, objects, etc.

2. Focus on the head of the verb. Define it as specifically as possible, then as abstractly as possible. What else could it mean?

3. See the head of this verb in your mind's eye as it would be written on the page. Notice if there's anything about the shape of the written word that reminds you of its definition. Does the shape resemble the action of this word?

4. Begin to silently mouth this verb. What do you learn about this word by the movement?

5. Where in your body does your relationship with this verb live? If you were to do this verb, what part of your body would have to activate first? If you would be unable to accomplish this verb, what sensations does that bring up for you?

6. Speak this word out loud while trying to vibrate that body part with your voice.

7. Are there any sensations, memories, dreams, or fears that you associate with this verb?

    a   If something comes up, speak the verb with that in mind.

    b   As if there were someone there to hear you, try to make them see and feel this image with just the word.

8. What would life be like if you could only do this verb?

9. What would life be like if you could never do this verb again?

10. Fold in all the modifiers attached to this verb. How do they specify this verb for you? Do they change the images coming to mind?

11. Take each modifier one by one.

    a   What other verbs could they modify? What would be their opposites?

    b   Speak the verb and this modifier with this new understanding.

LANGUAGE OF YOUR BODY

12 Say the whole thought that this verb belongs in. If you forget, notice what sensations that brings up and put them into the language as you make a thought up.

13 Rest and breathe. Let your mind wander around this verb and its modifiers.

14 Take a moment and write down anything new, surprising, or useful.

Whole thing

1 Whom is your character talking to?

2 What do they want from whomever they're speaking to?

3 How do they want them to feel?

4 Speak the whole text, noticing if the personalization exercise brought anything new to the performance.

5 Speak the whole text again, this time folding in all the skills from the previous chapter.

   a Know whom you're talking to and why.

   b Allow the personalization work to specify the images for you.

   c Be aware of where thoughts start and stop.

   d Let the function words be unimportant.

   e Keep your noun phrases together as all one thing and your verb phrases together as all one thing.

6 Speak the text again and let the work go. It'll be inside you somewhere. Just take flight.

You've brought the language into your body. Allow this deeper knowledge to inform the movement of the text. How does it physically feel to move through a noun within a larger noun phrase now that you know which specific nouns you mean? Why does your character choose to expand their thought in this way for the listener? Take your scene partner and the room into account. How is that reality affecting you and the language you're using? You're really in that room doing something. What does that bring up? If you make a mistake, notice the sensations in your body. They will affect how and why the next line of text comes out of you if you let them. If you have an actor thought like, "Ooooh, I messed up that thought," that's your character thinking they haven't gotten their point across; let it change how you move through the images, so your point comes out better.

Anything you do, feel, think, or say in this moment is happening to the character. Let it change you.

4
COLOR ME AWARE

Take a moment and notice the sensations of your scalp. This could include movement, how your hair feels, temperature, etc. Now gently scratch the entire surface of your scalp with your fingers or have a partner do it. Leave no corner unscratched. When the scratching ceases, notice the sensations of your scalp again. Anything new to report? Now fix your hair, if you have hair. Humans are capable of so much sensation, but we lose some awareness of the parts of us that we're not actively using, so that we're not distracted by overstimulation. That's why most of us aren't constantly aware of our pulse or our digestion or our scalp. When your scalp was scratched, suddenly the sensations there were more important. How about now? Can you still notice some sensations in your scalp that weren't there when you started? The sensations are probably starting to wane as your body readjusts to what it considers to be normal. If you were to consistently bring attention to your scalp, however, you could teach your body to be more aware of your scalp more often.

In the previous chapter, I asked you to be aware of quite a bit all at once while you were personalizing the text. You may have noticed your breath for a moment, the physical sensations of your body moving in space, the internal sensations of your emotional life. These are all sensations that can go by the wayside if we're not putting our attention on them consistently. The various disciplines that you study as an actor, however, are ways to build that awareness and turn it into a habit. Studying voice and singing will build your awareness of the breath and vibration of your bones. Movement, including the Alexander Technique, will build your awareness of your spine and the use of your body. Studying the art of clown will certainly bring awareness of the emotional sensations that move through you as you put yourself in front of people with a goal in mind. The more awareness of your physical self you bring to the text, the more alive that text will be when you personalize it. You'll have more sensation to learn from, and you'll be finely tuned to it, so it can affect your performance more easily. If you haven't yet, I highly recommend picking up the other titles in Acting Essentials series, so those experts can lead you toward your sensations in their special ways.

Here, we'll build and habituate your awareness of the physicality of speech—the act of transforming the images that live inside you into sound and sense. Now that you've explored what you say, you can become aware of how you say it. We'll start by visualizing the muscles, bones, cartilages, and open spaces of speech with a coloring book. From there we'll explore movement possibilities and how they affect the way you create sounds. This is a bit of a turning point. When you build your awareness of the anatomy of speech, the sounds that you employ to get what you need in the world or in performance will forever be a choice. You'll open up the possibility of changing your sound or reaffirming the sounds that you bring to the table. Whichever path you choose, the starting point is awareness.

COLOR ME AWARE

Play: Coloring!

In this section, you'll color the anatomy by number! For every image, there is a corresponding key on the opposite page. The key includes the name of the part of the anatomy, what letter it's labeled as in the image, and an empty box for you to fill in with the same color that you use for that part of the anatomy in the image. That way when you're looking for the mandible, you can find it in the key, see what color you've made it, and then locate it easily in the image. Some parts are labeled with the same letter, e.g., A1, A2, A3, etc. These are either separate sections of one whole part, or parts that work together to accomplish the same thing. You can color all of them shades of the same color, or if you have more than twenty-four distinct colors, you can color them all separately.

Key:

Bones

☐ A Mandible
☐ A1 Mandibular condyle
☐ B Temporal bone
☐ B1 Styloid process of temporal bone
☐ B2 Zygomatic process of temporal bone
☐ B3 Mastoid process of temporal bone
☐ C Zygomatic bone
☐ D Maxilla

Muscles that raise the mandible

☐ E Temporalis
☐ F Masseter

Muscles that lower the mandible

☐ G Medial pterygoid
☐ H Lateral pterygoid

When the jaw moves from open to closed, it's moving in two ways at the same time: straight up and down like an elevator, and on a diagonal like a swing. This allows the front teeth to separate farther than the molars can. To open the jaw, the pterygoids pull the mandibular condyle forward which sends the mandible down on an angle. The muscles of the jaw can also work together in different configurations to move the jaw in the directions needed for chewing.

1. Retraction—The back of the temporalis muscle can retract the jaw toward the spine.
2. Protrusion—The medial and lateral pterygoid muscles can work together to send the jaw forward, away from the spine.
3. Lateral—When the temporalis and medial and lateral pterygoids on one side of the head work together without their partners on the other side, they can move the jaw side to side.

COLOR ME AWARE

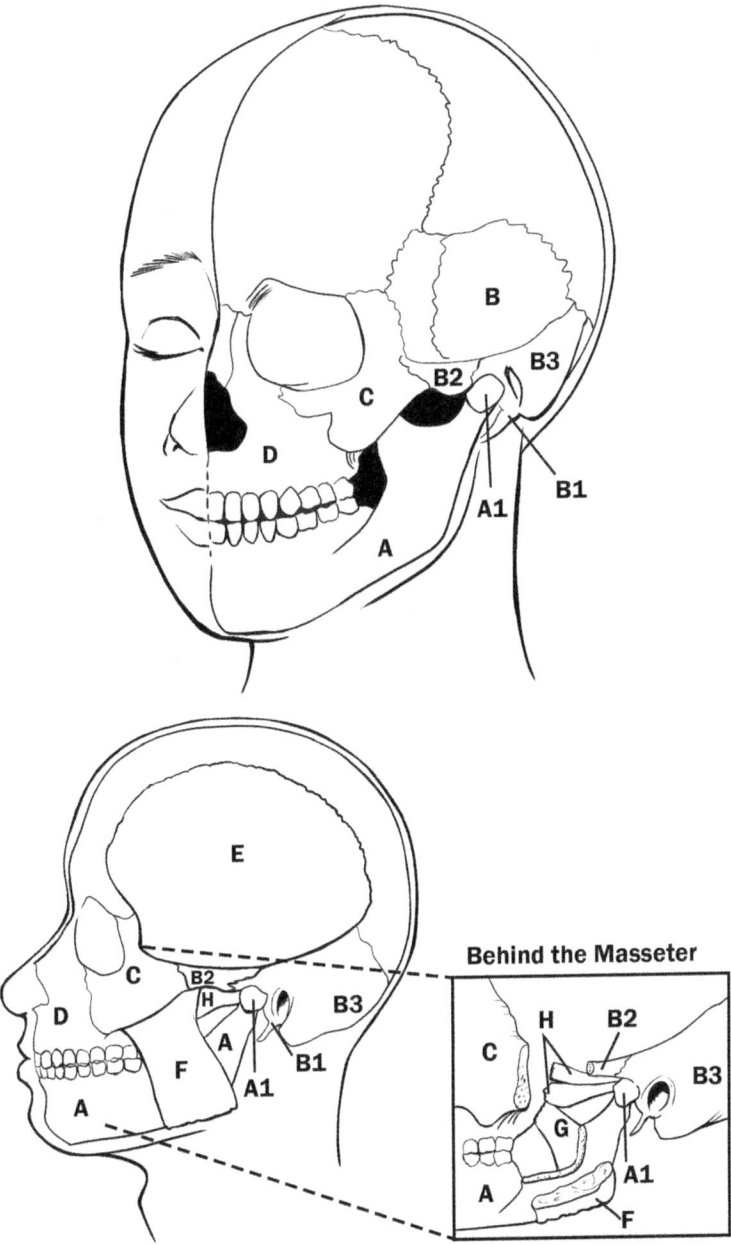

FIGURE 1 The skull and jaw.

Key:

☐ A Mandible
☐ B Occipital Bone
☐ B1 Mastoid process of temporal bone
☐ C Spine
☐ D Clavicle (collar bone)
☐ E Scapula (shoulder blade)
☐ E1 Acromion of the scapula

Muscles that move lips toward each other

☐ F Orbicularis oris

Muscles that spread the lip corners

☐ G Buccinator
☐ H Risorius

Muscles that raise the upper lip

☐ I Levator labii superior
☐ J Levator labii inferiorus
☐ K Zygomaticus minor
☐ L Zygomaticus major
☐ M Levator anguli oris

Nose muscle

☐ N Nasalis

Muscles of the bottom lip and chin

☐ O Mentalis
☐ P1 Depressor anguli oris
☐ P2 Depressor anguli inferiorus
☐ P3 Platysma

Muscles of the eyes and eyebrows

☐ Q1 Frontalis
☐ Q2 Procerus
☐ R Orbicularis oculi

Muscles of the neck, shoulder, and back

☐ S Trapezius
☐ T Levator scapula
☐ U Sternocleidomastoid
☐ U1 Scalenes

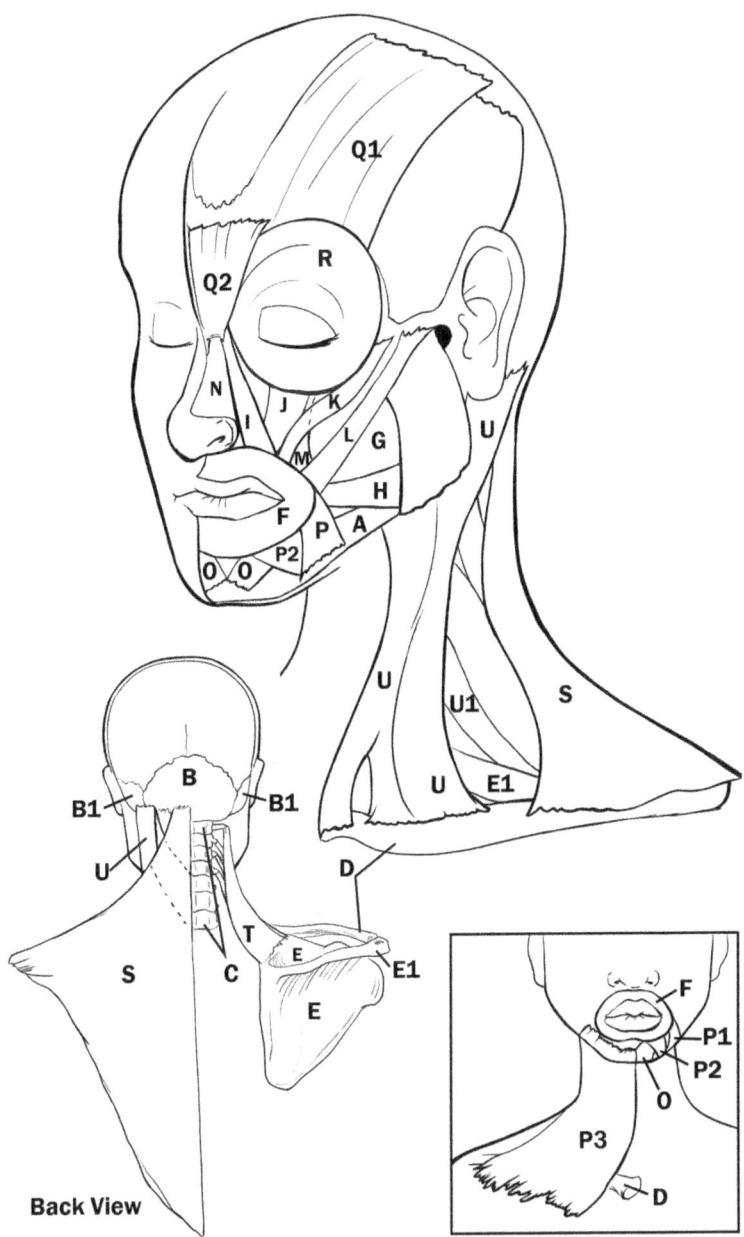

FIGURE 2 Muscles of the face.

Key:

Important structures near the larynx

- ☐ A Mandible
- ☐ B Clavicle
- ☐ C Trachea ("windpipe")
- ☐ D Styloid process of temporal bone
- ☐ E Acromion of the scapula
- ☐ F Hyoid bone*

The larynx itself

- ☐ G Thyroid cartilage**
- ☐ H Cricoid cartilage
- ☐ I Arytenoid cartilage
- ☐ J Vocal folds ("vocal cords")
- ☐ J1 Vestibular folds*** ("false folds")
- ☐ K Glottis
- ☐ L Epiglottis

- ☐ M *Muscles that lower the larynx*
- ☐ M1 Sternohyoid
- ☐ M2 Omohyoid
- ☐ M3 Mylohyoid
- ☐ M4 Geniohyoid
- ☐ M5 Thyrohyoid
- ☐ O *Muscles that open the pharynx (throat)*
- ☐ O1 Stylopharyngeus
- ☐ Palatopharyngeus (pictured in next figure)
- ☐ P *Muscles that close the pharynx*
- ☐ P1 Superior pharyngeal constrictor
- ☐ P2 Medial pharyngeal constrictor
- ☐ P3 Inferior pharyngeal constrictor

Note: * The hyoid is the only bone in the body that is not directly attached to any other bone. It acts as a connector for the muscles of the larynx, pharynx (throat), and tongue.

** The thyroid cartilage is sometimes called the "Adam's apple." While present in all sexes, it's more visible in people with male secondary sex characteristics.

*** The vestibular folds, sometimes called the "false folds," are above the vocal folds. They're used to help us not choke when we swallow and in certain singing styles to create a second pitch.

COLOR ME AWARE

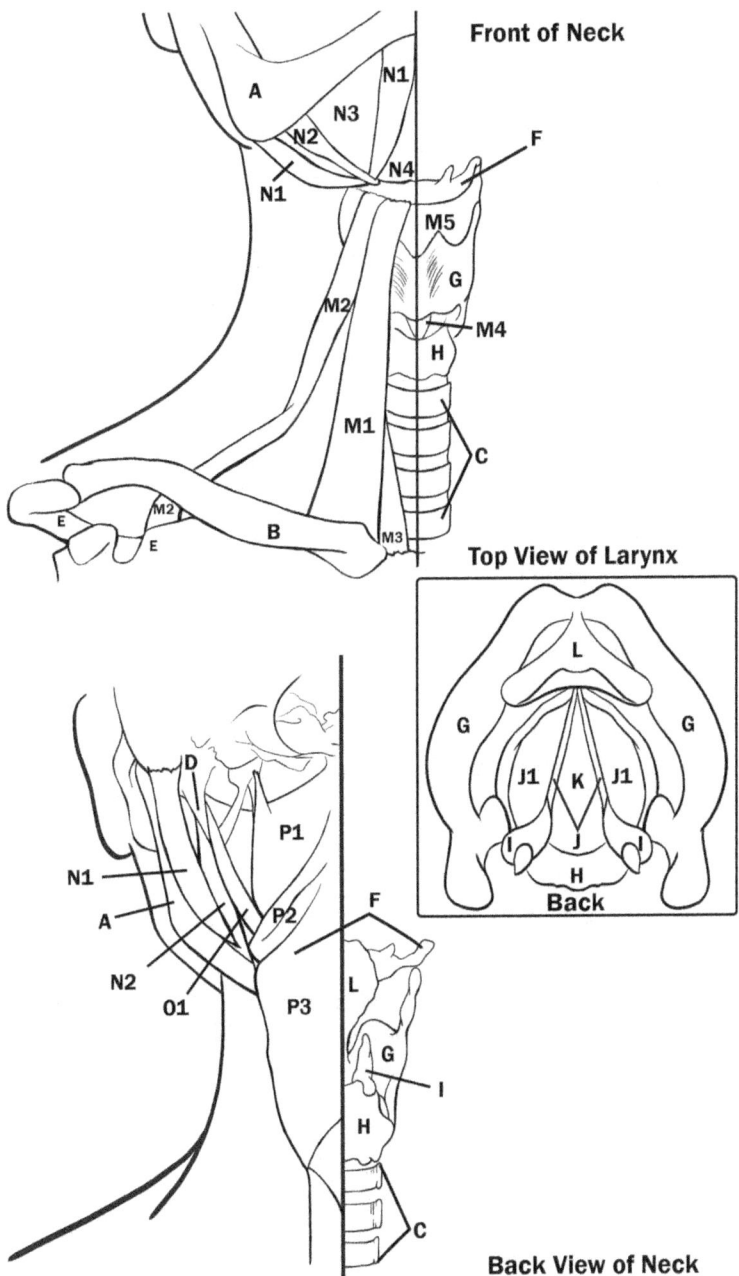

FIGURE 3 The larynx.

INTRODUCTION TO SPEECHWORK FOR ACTORS

Key:
- A Mandible
- B Trachea
- C Esophagus

Open Spaces
- D Sinus
- E Nasal cavity
- F Oral cavity
- G1 Nasopharynx
- G2 Oropharynx
- G3 Laryngopharynx

Larynx
- H Glottis
- I Hyoid Bone
- J Epiglottis*
- K Thyroid cartilage
- L Arytenoid cartilage
- M Cricoid cartilage

Articulators
- N Lips
- O1 Tip of the tongue (apex)
- O2 Blade of the tongue (lamina)
- O3 Front of the body of the tongue
- O4 Middle of the body of the tongue
- O5 Back of the body of the tongue
- O6 Tongue root
- P Velum (soft palate)
- Q Uvula
- R Vocal folds
- S Teeth
- T Alveolar ridge
- U Postalveolar palate
- V Palate (hard palate)

Muscles that open the pharynx
- P1 Palatopharyngeus (part of the velum)

*The parts of the anatomy that make contact with one another to create phonemes are called articulators. Moveable articulators change their shape to act on each other or on the immovable articulators, which do not change their shape.

**Fun fact!* For our purposes, I've labeled the epiglottis, which is a flap that covers the larynx for swallowing, as part of the larynx, but there are rare languages that use the epiglottis as an articulator.

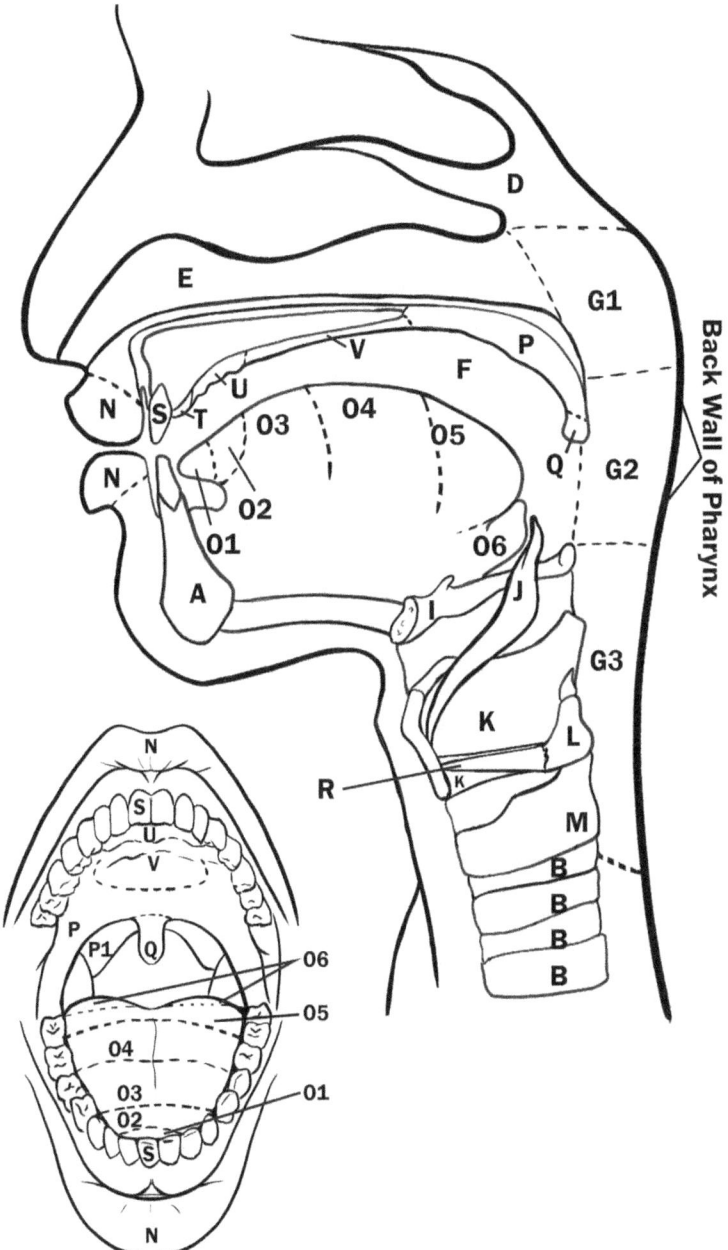

FIGURE 4 The vocal tract and articulators.

5
THE WORK OF AWARENESS

Learning about the speech anatomy and distinguishing one part from another is a great first step in building awareness of your speech. We'll go into even more detail later in this chapter about how you use each part to create speech sounds. The kind of *physical* awareness that we're after, however, requires a bit more work. Building awareness is a practice—something that requires consistent attention to maintain.

I like to break the goals of practice down into the short game and the long game. In the short game, you have a task like a sonnet or a rap, so you do a series of exercises that will prepare your mouth for the task, which you then do multiple times until it comes out right. You practice. The long game—or a practice—is the slow and methodical way you train your body for new habits and then continue to apply those skills purposefully. A practice takes upkeep. The more of the long game you play, the easier it will be to "get in the zone" in your short game. In other words, the more time you spend fine-tuning your awareness of the speech muscles as a general practice, the less time you will need to spend on warming up when you have a performance task. There are many long-game practices that you might already be aware of: the ballet bar, martial arts forms, musical instrument drills, yoga, etc. In these activities, you train your body and mind through a series of mindful, sometimes repetitive exercises that build the required skills for that activity. Then, when you have an opponent rushing you, or it's your turn to improvise a jazz lick, your muscles are able to respond with skill and poise, because your body remembers what to do from the drills.

In order to get the muscles of speech primed for such spontaneity, my practice includes exercises that help them *release, isolate,* and *activate.*

Release exercises are the massages and stretches that will help you gain flexibility by letting the muscles that don't need to work relax and stay out of the way. Sometimes, extraneous muscle use—what some call tension—can even be an underlying factor in the formation of medical issues such as vocal nodules or temporomandibular joint syndrome (TMJ). We don't want to exacerbate those kinds of issues by strengthening the muscular imbalances that can lead to them, so before we exercise, we want to limber up. After release, I move into isolation drills to wake up the muscles that I want to be working without using extra tension to accomplish the same movement. Last, I activate the muscles of speech by incorporating sounds, words, and thoughts that challenge specific skills. I liken this to the across-the-floor section of a dance class or shooting drills and batting practice. Once your speech is primed in this manner, you can begin bringing your imagination into the game.

In the following sections, you will learn the warm-ups that I use in class. Feel free to visit the companion videos in Appendix D to follow along. Once you get the hang of the exercises, going through the whole warm-up should take half an hour to an hour, depending on your speed. It's a workout. I recommend doing a speech workout at least twice a week while you're actively training. On off days, pick and choose exercises to create your own ten- to fifteen-minute daily warm-up that challenges the skills that you need more practice with. You can use the same template to build a short-game warm-up to do before any rehearsal or performance opportunity. Combine these with a voice warm-up and you'll be cooking with gas! If you move through all of Acting Essentials, you'll feel how each discipline is connected to the next so you can create your own templates for short-game and long-game warm-ups that prepare your whole system for embodied performance.

Release

This is a series of stretches and massages to release the musculature of speech and the surrounding areas while building your awareness. You can either give yourself a complete release by going through the entire series, or select a few exercises from each section as part of your daily practice.

THE WORK OF AWARENESS

Muscles of expression

1. Gently tap your face, scalp, and neck to encourage blood flow and awareness.
2. Use your fingertips to move your scalp around on your skull like you're getting a great professional shampoo. Can you let your jaw hang open while you work?
3. Massage your forehead from your eyebrows to where your unicorn horn would be.
4. Rub your hands together to warm them up and gently place them over your eyes. Hold for twenty seconds. Feel the muscles release.
5. Stretching and squishing:
   a. Stretch every muscle of your face outward and hold while making whatever noise you think fits this look.
   b. Squish every muscle of your face inward and hold while making whatever noise you think fits this look.
   c. Stretch the top half of your face and squish the bottom half of your face and make whatever noise fits this look.
   d. Stretch the bottom half of your face and squish the top half of your face and make whatever noise fits this look.
   e. Go back and forth between steps c and d as quickly as you can.
   f. Stretch the right half of your face and squish the left half of your face and make whatever noise fits this look.
   g. Stretch the left half of your face and squish the right half of your face and make whatever noise fits this look.
   h. Go back and forth between steps f and g as quickly as you can.
   i. Try diagonals! Good luck! This is where my brain breaks.
6. Drop your head forward and gently shake your face. Make some noise while you do.

Neck and throat

When working with your neck, it's very important to listen to your body. If a stretch feels like it's too much, it probably is—ease off a little bit. It's not useful to stretch something so much that other parts of your body have to tense up to accommodate it. The goal isn't to pull the neck into a new shape, but to allow gravity to help you find length and a light stretch.

1. Side stretch (trapezius, scalenes):

   a. Without leaning to one side, drop an ear toward your right shoulder and breathe.

   b. This may be a pretty intense stretch as it is, but if not, you can drape your right arm over your head and let the weight of that arm aid your stretch.

   c. You may be lifting your right shoulder accidentally. To release it, lift your shoulder toward your ear and gently drop it back down.

   d. Reach your resting, left arm down toward the floor with the palm facing in, then with the palm facing out.

   e. When this stretch feels finished, drop your arm, then drop your chin to your chest to roll your head to the left side. Repeat this stretch on your left side.

2. Skunk stripe (side of the trapezius):

   a. Without leaning, drop your right ear toward your right shoulder and breathe.

   b. Rotate your head so your nose points easily toward your right armpit.

   c. Drape your right arm over your head like a skunk stripe and hold while you breathe.

   d. When this stretch feels finished, drop your arm, roll your chin to your chest, and repeat this stretch on your left side.

3. Ceiling secrets (levator scapulae):

   a. Drop your chin to your chest.

   b. With your head dropped, rotate your right ear toward the ceiling and your chin toward your right shoulder.

THE WORK OF AWARENESS

    c   Drape the left arm over your head.

    d   Use the right arm to gently push against an imaginary wall behind you and breathe.

    e   When this stretch feels finished, drop your arm, then drop your chin to your chest to repeat on the other side.

4   Chin to chest (upper trapezius):

    a   Keeping your torso tall, drop your chin to your chest.

    b   Clasp your hands behind your head and release your elbows to let the weight of your arms aid your stretch

    c   Using your hands instead of your neck muscles, turn your nose back and forth from your right armpit to your left.

    d   Come back to center and use your hands to push your head back up.

5   Piano strings (scalenes):

    a   Walk your fingers in the pressure points where your clavicles meet your neck.

    b   You may feel taut stringy muscles. Gently press into them on each side.

    c   Gently close your jaw and lift your chin and use it to paint a rainbow on the ceiling.

    d   Bring your chin down, move your fingers to the next stringy muscle, and repeat.

6   SCM (sternocleidomastoid) massage:

    a   Touch the spot on your neck where your collarbones meet your sternum—the sternoclavicular notch.

    b   Turn your head right and feel the muscle that pops out on the left side—the SCM.

    c   Trace the SCM with your fingers. It goes all the way up behind your ear.

    d   Pinch the SCM so you don't lose it, then turn your head to the left to relax it.

    e Massage the SCM by pinching it all the way from your collarbone to your skull.

    f Repeat on the other side.

7. Place your fingers on either side of your larynx and gently move it to the left and right.
8. Rub your hands together to warm them up, then wrap them around your neck and hold for a deep release.
9. Gently roll your head from shoulder to shoulder across your chest, paying extra attention to the crunchy spots. Bring your head back up on top of your shoulders.

Jaw

Unless otherwise noted, the goal here is to allow your jaw to relax and hang open. Like the neck, the jaw is a delicate creature. When massaging and manipulating the jaw, go easy! If you feel pain or hear popping, pause the exercise and visit a doctor. A massage can be a kneading motion with the fingertips, or you can apply gentle pressure and drag your fingers across the muscle. Try both!

1. Temple massage (temporalis):

    a To find the temporalis, place your hands on the side of your head and gently clench your jaw. Now stop that! This muscle is located where you feel muscle movement.

    b Massage from your temples to all the places you felt this muscle move on the sides of your head.

    c For extra release, gently tug your ears in all directions while letting your jaw hang.

2. Cheek massage (masseter):

    a To find the masseter, place your hands on your cheeks under your ears and gently clench your jaw. Release that. This muscle is located where you feel movement.

    b Massage from your cheekbones to your chin where you felt this muscle move.

THE WORK OF AWARENESS 65

3 Chin strap release (pterygoids):
  a Place one hand behind your head.
  b With the thumb and forefinger of the other hand make a cup around your jaw.
  c Using your hands, gently push your jaw two millimeters back toward your spine.
  d Hold and breathe for a moment, then release.
  e Trace your thumbs up the back of your mandible to the spot behind your earlobe.
  f Gently press your thumbs inward toward each other and forward toward your jaw.
  g Breathe and hold for a moment, then release. Oh, the sweet, sweet succor of release.

4 Dudley Knight's all-purpose jaw release:
  a Press your thumbs into the back of your mandible behind your ears.
  b Press the four fingers of each hand to the top of your temporalis muscle above your ears in a fan shape.
  c Apply gentle pressure into your temporalis as you drag your thumbs down the shape of the mandible.
  d When your thumbs reach the angle of the mandible, allow your fingers to come to the bottom of your cheekbones.
  e Apply gentle pressure to your masseter muscles as you drag your thumbs down and forward along the mandible. It should feel like you're gently pulling your jaw open with your hands.
  f Repeat this exercise and make sure that your jaw isn't fighting back, but allowing itself to be gently opened by your hands.

5 Grab your chin with both hands and wiggle it straight up and down. If your teeth are clacking together or you're afraid of what might happen if they did, try loosely sticking your tongue between them as a cushion.

6. Let your jaw drop with gravity then close it with your hand. Be sure it's your hand that's closing the jaw and not your jaw muscles.
7. Rub your hands together to warm them up and then cradle your jaw in your warm hands.

Lips

1. Lip muscle (orbicularis oris):
    a. Blow through your lips like a horse. Then repeat while adding voice.
    b. Massage between your upper lip and nose and between your lower lip and chin.
    c. Massage your lip corners.
    d. Stretch your lips in every direction with your pinkies.
2. Cheek release (buccinator):
    a. Place the heels of your hands on your masseter muscles under your cheekbones and apply gentle pressure.
    b. Drag the heels of your hands down your masseters and manually open your jaw.
    c. When the heels of your hands are between your teeth, apply inward pressure and slide your hands forward to drag your thumbs across your cheeks.
3. Drop your head forward and shake out your lips.

Tongue

1. Blow through your tongue like you're blowing raspberries at someone.
2. Keep the tip of your tongue glued to your lower front teeth while you stretch the middle of your tongue over your lip.
3. Massage the underside of your chin with your thumb. This can help release the tongue root.

THE WORK OF AWARENESS

4 Without moving your jaw from side to side, trace the tip of your tongue along the inside of your teeth. If that is easy, graduate to the sharp edges, and then the outside of your teeth.

5 Drop your head and shake your tongue while making the noise of release.

Velum

1 The professional yawn is an exercise that I love because I can really feel the hard-to-massage back of my tongue and pharynx stretching. Sticking out your tongue and yawning with abandon takes some getting used to, especially in a classroom setting, but it's oh so worth it when you do.

    a Yawn the way you habitually do and notice the movement of your tongue.

    b This time when you yawn, fight against that natural movement and stretch your tongue all the way out like a cat.

    c Feel free to make a gentle yawn noise.

2 Exploding and imploding "Ks":

    a Make a "K" sound and continue exhaling for three seconds after.

    b Repeat the "K" motion while inhaling, and continue to inhale for three seconds.

    c Try to make your inhales and exhales as quiet as possible.

    d Go back and forth between exploding and imploding "Ks" until another yawn comes. When it does, make it professional.

Isolate

Think of speech like ballroom dancing. Even though you know the basic steps to your favorite dance, without practice you may add extra movements from other styles or engage parts of your body that you may not need to. By studying the dance steps in isolation, you can then recombine them to merengue or foxtrot with your partner. These exercises are the dance moves for speech. By practicing the movements in isolation, you'll have a greater awareness of how you personally recombine them. You'll also be opening up possibilities for combining them in different styles. As you work on the following exercises, check out each muscle you're isolating in the coloring section (Chapter 4) and in a mirror. That way you'll connect what you see in the images to what you see and feel in your own body. You can either work on the entire series or add a few exercises to your daily practice, depending on your speech goals.

Jaw

To begin these exercises, shake out your head and then let your jaw drop in response to the pull of gravity. If you feel (or see in the mirror) that you're using muscles to actively place your jaw into this position, repeat the jaw-release exercises and try to let the jaw just fall to where it falls. As you isolate the muscles of the jaw, pay attention to how the jaw rebounds to its released, no-muscles state. Learn to love this no-muscles feeling. Full disclosure: the jaw often does way more work than it needs to during speech, and one of my main goals for my practice is to give my jaw a break by strengthening the other speech muscles and getting them to do their share. We'll begin this section by isolating the movements of the jaw, so that you'll be able to recognize any of these movements creeping in while you're isolating the rest of the anatomy. When that happens, you can just reset your jaw to its released, no-muscles position and start the isolation again. As we go through the jaw exercises, we're not looking for the extremes of these movements. Be gentle.

1. Closing (temporalis and masseter muscles): lift the jaw until your teeth gently touch, then drop the jaw to reset.
2. Opening (lateral pterygoids): gently open the jaw. Let the jaw relax and spring back up to the no-muscles place.
3. Protrusion (medial and lateral pterygoids): gently move your jaw forward away from your spine. Release and feel the jaw spring back.

THE WORK OF AWARENESS

4 Retraction (temporalis): gently move your jaw backward toward your spine. Release and feel the jaw spring forward.

5 Lateral (medial and lateral pterygoids activated one side at a time): *keep this movement small*. Gently move your jaw to one side and release to the no-muscles position. Repeat the movement to the other side and release.

Now that you've built some awareness of what jaw activation feels like, you can move on to isolating and strengthening the articulators. Start slowly and deliberately enough to listen to your body. Be sure the jaw doesn't get involved. You can use your mirror to keep yourself honest. If you feel your jaw beginning to take over, you can place your hands on your cheeks as a reminder to keep it released. When you can perform the exercises without the jaw, you can start to drill those movements. I like to repeat these movements ten times in a row or in a fun rhythm to help me get faster and faster with each isolation.

Lips

1 Spreading (risorius): bring your lip corners straight back toward your ears and then release.

2 Trumpeting (outer orbicularis oris): move your lips forward like the bell of a trumpet and release. Did your jaw stay relaxed?

3 Pursing (inner orbicularis oris): bring your lips in toward each other. Make sure the lip corners are moving in too.

4 Raising (levators): lift your upper lip toward your nose like you smell something awful.

5 Depressing (depressors): lower your bottom lip toward your chin like a sad clown.

6 Pause to play!

    a Can you do all these movements on one side while the other side stays relaxed?

    b The aside: spread one side of your lips while trumpeting the other.

c The fishy face: hold your lips forward in a trumpet shape, then purse and release. It helps if you make fins with your hands.

d What other funny faces can you make by mixing and matching these isolations? Can you do these with a relaxed jaw?

Cheeks

1 Bracing (buccinators): Move your cheeks inward toward your teeth. I feel this movement right behind my lip corners. Alternate route: Blow through your lips like a horse. Can you feel your lip corners working? This is the action of the buccinators. Try isolating that same movement without the horse noises.

2 Smiling (zygomaticus): Smile your biggest, toothiest smile.

a Release the lip corners without releasing the muscles around your cheekbones, the zygomaticus muscles.

b Release your cheeks and then activate the zygomaticus without the smile this time.

c Alternate route: Imagine that the sun's in your eyes and raise your cheeks to lessen the effects. It helps if you put your hand between you and the sun to create shade.

Tongue

We've made it to the tongue—the star of the articulation show. I know it's tempting to let the jaw help, but the tongue can and will do these movements unassisted. The tongue is all muscle, and its fibers run in multiple directions, which allows the tongue to move in a variety of ways. The longitudinal muscles are the fibers that run the long way on your tongue—from the tip to the back. When some fibers contract and others release, the tongue curls up, down, left, or right. If they all contract at the same time, the tongue retracts back into itself like a nervous turtle. The verticalis fibers run vertically from the top to the bottom of your tongue. When they contract, your tongue flattens and widens to the sides like a pancake. The transversus fibers run across the tongue from side to side. When they contract, the sides of the tongue move in toward each other, which makes the tongue tall and thick. These movements can be combined in different ways or performed in one part of the tongue and not another, which is how we create arcs or cups in the tongue. The "tongue root" is an umbrella term we use for the way back of the tongue, which comprises the hyoglossus, styloglossus, and genioglossus. The tongue root can be used to move the tongue forward and back like a conveyor belt. These muscles are also very important for swallowing. As a reminder, neither your jaw nor your lips need to do any work while you isolate the tongue. If using your lips or jaw helps you find the movement at first, go right ahead, but then keep exploring until you can isolate these movements of the tongue without the extra work from the lips and jaw.

1   Curling (superior and anterior longitudinal muscles): stick your tongue out forward.

    a   Move the tip of your tongue up toward your nose, then move the tip of your tongue down toward your chin.

    b   Move the tip of your tongue to the left and then to the right.

    c   Move your tongue in circles around the outside of your lips without using your jaw.

2   Flattening (verticalis): press the sides of your tongue into your bottom molars to make your tongue flat and wide like a pancake.

3   Bunching (transversus): bring the sides of your tongue in toward each other to make your tongue tall and thick like a sausage. Alternate route: Bite the center of your tongue and then use the muscles of your tongue to pry your teeth apart.

4   Grooving (styloglossus): raise the sides of your tongue to make a shape like a hotdog bun, pita, or aqueduct.

5   Tongue root retracting (styloglossus, hyoglossus): bring your tongue straight back toward your spine like it's on a conveyor belt. You should feel this motion starting at the way back of the tongue.

6   Tongue root advancing (genioglossus): slide your tongue forward. Keep your tongue as released as possible. You should feel this motion starting at the very back of your tongue.

The next two tongue isolations go a bit beyond the faces a child might make in the mirror. They take concentration and a bit more trial and error. These exercises, however, are the building blocks of many speech sounds, so mastering these motions will make your explorations of sounds later in the book more robust. I recommend putting a two-minute exploration of both of these exercises into your daily practice until you can do them on command. From then a quick check-in with these motions will do the trick.

7   Arching (transversus, palatoglossus): while keeping the tip of your tongue touching the back of the lower front teeth, bunch different sections of your tongue until they touch the roof of your mouth while the rest of the tongue stays relaxed and low. This is how we make certain sounds, like "K."

  a   Roll the arch from the front to the back of your tongue and then to the front again.

  b   When that becomes easy, try rolling an arch from front to back with enough space between your tongue and the roof of your mouth to breathe though.

  c   **Pro Tip:** Rolling the arch is the action that changes the pitch while whistling.

8   Cupping (hyoglossus, verticalis, transversus, longitudinals, palatoglossus): while keeping the tip of your tongue touching the lower front teeth, make a small groove with different sections of your tongue like a cup or bowl that could hold a drop of water.

  a   Make a cup in the front of your tongue, then roll the cup to the back of your tongue and then to the front again.

  b   **Pro Tip:** If you're struggling, place a blueberry on your tongue and hold it there by letting your tongue form an indentation the blueberry can sit in. Then roll the blueberry from front to back. Hold your breath so you don't choke.

Velum

The **velum**, or soft palate, is made up of a group of muscles in the back of the roof of the mouth that lower to open the pathway to the nose or raise to close off the pathway to the nose (nasopharyngeal

THE WORK OF AWARENESS

port). It's like an attic door that leads to the nasal cavity. I love using a mirror and a flashlight to peek into my mouth during these isolations. It's really amazing how unconsciously coordinated our bodies are even when doing relatively simple tasks like breathing.

1. Isolating the velum:
    a. Snort loudly. That feeling in the back of your mouth or nose is your soft palate wiggling. That's where we're working.
    b. Breathe through your mouth only. You can use your hand to feel under your nose to make sure no air is escaping. Notice what the velum and the tongue are doing.
    c. Without closing your mouth, and keeping the back of your tongue relatively relaxed, switch to breathing just through your nose. Notice what the velum and the tongue are doing.
    d. Switch back and forth without closing your mouth. Don't forget to look in the mirror to see your velum moving.
    e. Inhale and exhale through your mouth and nose at the same time. Notice where your velum is.
    f. Switch back and forth between breathing through your nose and mouth together and breathing through your mouth alone. Notice the movement of your velum.
    g. When you get good at controlling the motion of the velum, you can begin to lift and release it without breathing in and out. Try bobbing your velum while holding your breath.
    h. **Pro Tip:** If this isn't coming naturally, think of preparing to breathe through your mouth, then preparing to breathe through both your nose and mouth. The way your body adjusts is by moving the velum. Then just do that faster and faster.
    i. When you get good at bobbing your velum on purpose, try it with your lips closed.
2. Sounding with the velum:
    a. Hold out an "NG" sound.
    b. Slide from "NG" to "AH" as slowly as you can. Feel your tongue and your velum separate. How far apart can you get them and what does that sound like?

c Slide from "AH" to "NG" as slowly as you can. Feel your tongue and velum move together. When they're close, how slowly can you move before they actually touch?

Larynx and glottis

The **larynx**, also known as the voice box, is a movable cartilage structure that sits in the front of the neck. The larynx connects the *trachea*, the windpipe from the lungs, to the throat, mouth, and nose. Gently press your finger underneath your chin, then trace it down the front of your throat until you feel a small dip like the pour spout on a measuring bowl. That dip is the top of your *thyroid cartilage*, the large, shield-like cartilage that protects the larynx from the front. The hard structure that you passed on the way to the dip (that is now just above and behind your finger) is the *hyoid bone*. The horseshoe-shaped hyoid bone is the only free-floating bone in the body, and the attached muscles connect it to the larynx, tongue, soft palate, skull, clavicles, and even shoulder blades! The muscles lift and lower the hyoid bone (which moves the larynx) to aid in breathing, swallowing, and of course speech. Swallow with your finger in the dip of the thyroid cartilage to feel what I mean.

Right below your finger, attached to the inside of the thyroid cartilage, are your **vocal folds** or vocal cords, a set of two bands of muscle tissue in the larynx used for phonation. In the back of the larynx, the vocal folds attach to the pyramid-shaped *arytenoid cartilages* to form a triangular opening called the **glottis**. The arytenoids are rotated by their muscles to bring the folds together or apart and can tilt toward or away from the thyroid cartilage. When the vocal folds are open, air is allowed to pass freely through them so we can breathe. When they're closed, air can't move through them. When air is allowed to travel through the vocal folds while they are close together, the change of pressure makes them undulate, so the air passes through in quick puffs, creating the vibration we hear as pitch. This pitch is the voice, and the vibration that creates it is called **phonation**.

The pitch of the voice can be changed by changing the length of the vocal folds. The vocal folds attach in the front to the thyroid cartilage and in the back to the arytenoid cartilages. These structures sit atop the *cricoid cartilage*, which acts as a stable base to allow them to move in relation to one another. When we move the arytenoid and thyroid

THE WORK OF AWARENESS

cartilages apart, the vocal folds become taut, creating a higher pitch. When the structures move toward one another, the vocal folds loosen and the pitch goes down.

The following isolations will take you through some of the ways we use our vocal folds while speaking. These are things that many of us do all the time when we speak without being fully aware of it. If it feels like you can't do something, make a note of it and come back to it after you explore other aspects of your speech. Chances are, you'll catch yourself doing some of these actions eventually, and then you can come back to making the actions purposeful.

1. Opening and closing the vocal folds:
   a. Breathe through your mouth. When you're breathing, your vocal folds are open.
   b. Keeping your mouth open, take a deep breath and hold it. You likely just closed your vocal folds.
   c. Release your breath. You likely just opened your vocal folds. Maybe you even felt the air pop through them.
   d. Do all that again, but this time when you release the air, exhale slowly and start and stop the flow of air to make a string of popping noises like a quiet cough. The spot where you feel the pop is where your vocal folds contact each other.
   e. **Pro Tip:** Quickly whisper "uh-oh" ten times for the same effect and notice the tiny popping feeling.
2. Whisper:
   a. Breathe silently through your mouth.
   b. Without moving your tongue or velum, make that breath audible, like a light "H" sound. You have likely just brought your vocal folds into close proximity without making contact, so we can hear the air as it travels through the glottis.
   c. **Whisper** a sentence. We can articulate without our vocal folds making contact, but we lose some details of speech—namely the difference between voiced and voiceless sounds.

3   Creaky voice:

   a   Starting with your vocal folds gently closed, slowly send a small stream of air through them and out of your mouth. If you go slowly enough, you might feel something like Pop Rocks in your throat. If it sounds like a creaky door, you're doing it.

   b   Try making this sound a bit louder. This type of voicing is called **creaky voice**, or **vocal fry**, and it's used in many languages and accents. Be careful: if you're speaking a language like Vietnamese, if you say the same syllable with or without creaky voice, you'll change the meaning of the whole word!

   c   Speak a sentence! Does this feel familiar at all?

4   Modal voice, or "full phonation":

   a   Find creaky voice again, and slowly speed up the air until you hear a pitch. This easy stream of pitch is called "full phonation," "full voice," or **modal voice**. Your vocal folds are close together, so the air passing through them makes them undulate against each other, which breaks up the flow of air into pulses that we hear as pitch.

   b   Speak a sentence in modal voice. Does this feel familiar? Is it easy to stay in modal voice for the entire thought, or do you slip into creaky voice or something like a whisper?

5   Breathy voice:

   a   Begin speaking in a whisper.

   b   Add a bit of pitch to that whisper so you're halfway from a whisper to modal voice. This is called **breathy voice**, or a stage whisper, off voice, or sometimes sotto voce. When we speak in breathy voice, part of our vocal folds is undulating to create pitch while another section is being held apart, so air passes through in a stream and a pulse.

Conceptualizing this part changed the game for me. I think this is a beautiful example of where science and art intertwine. The vocal folds are somewhere between one thumbnail and one thumb pad long,

THE WORK OF AWARENESS

way too small to single-handedly create the sound that we call voice. When you have the impulse to say something, you bring your vocal folds together and send breath through them to create the pulses of air that we hear as pitch, while the articulators create the shapes we hear as speech. The pulses from the vocal folds vibrate the cartilage of the larynx, molecule by molecule, in a wave. The round shapes of the larynx, hyoid bone, mouth, nose, and skull amplify some parts of that wave and dampen others. This wave of vibration is shaped by the specific shape of your bones, which are unlike the specific shape of anyone else's.

If your muscles are tight around the bones while they're vibrating, they will mute that vibration like a thumb resting on a guitar string. You might hear voice teachers talk about a natural voice, or vocal freedom. Releasing the unnecessary tension that keeps your bones from vibrating at their fullest is a big part of that work. When your bones are really ringing, new impulses or emotions will change the shape of the wave of vibration. Then your wave of vibration leaves your body. Outside of you, your sound wave—which only your body can make—vibrates each molecule of air until it lands in someone's ear and vibrates their tympanic membrane. The eardrum turns that wave into electrical impulse, and somehow the brain understands that electricity as language. But that wave—your voice, your shape—isn't just hitting their ears. It vibrates their skin, their eyes, their heart center. Something changed in you to give you an impulse to speak, so you took a breath and sent your shape out of you as vibration and physically affected someone. It's acoustics, physiology, communication, and art. When you want to woo, annoy, cajole, soothe, or uplift someone, your voice acts on them physically. This book is about exploring all the ways we can safely shape this vibration into language in a relaxed, flexible way so that more of your vibration—more of *you*—can be involved when you communicate. It starts with this concept.

1 Vibration exploration:
    a Walk around the room putting your body on different surfaces and objects while making voice. Yes, go hug things.
    b Notice how different surfaces respond to your vibration.
    c Play in the different registers: whisper, creaky voice, breathy voice, modal voice.

- d Play with pitch. Different objects will respond to different pitches.
- e If you have access to a piano, open it so you can see the strings, then press the sustain pedal so the hammers come off of the strings. Say "AH" into the piano and the strings will vibrate your voice back to you.

2 Pitch:
- a Place your hand on your larynx to feel if the thyroid cartilage moves.
- b With a relaxed jaw, tongue, and lips, slide your pitch as high as it goes, then slide your pitch as low as it goes.
- c Notice if your larynx moves. When it's not moving, that means the arytenoid muscles are doing all the work for that pitch change. When it does move, it means that the thyroid cartilage has gotten involved for that pitch change.
- d Try moving your pitch in the different registers: whisper, creaky voice, breathy voice, and modal voice.
    - i Notice what changing your pitch feels like in each register.
    - ii Changing pitch is easier in some registers than in others. Which register gives you the broadest range of pitch?

Pharynx

The **pharynx** is the name for the area in the back of the nose, mouth, and throat (nasopharynx, oropharynx, and laryngopharynx, respectively). One set of muscles is used to constrict, or shrink, these areas, and another is used to expand them. Both processes are useful in swallowing and speech.

1 Expanding the nasopharynx:
- a Breathe through your nose with your jaw and tongue relaxed. Feel the path of the cool air as it moves from the nose down the throat. The shapes you feel are the boundaries of the nasopharynx and maybe some of the oropharynx.

THE WORK OF AWARENESS

- **b** On your next exhale, allow some voice to move through that shape. It'll be a gentle hum.
- **c** Imagine you have your favorite flower, plate of food, or person in front of you. As you inhale through your nose, try to smell your image. If you have no sense of smell, imagine the pool of cool air in the back of your nose getting wider.
- **d** On your next exhale, allow some voice to move through that shape. Did your hum change?

2 Expanding the oropharynx (stylopharyngeus, palatopharyngeus):
- **a** Gently open your mouth and breathe through your mouth and nose at the same time. Feel the path of the cool air as it moves through the nose, mouth, and throat.
- **b** On your next exhale, gently send some voice through that shape. Be mindful that you don't change the shape in an effort to "make voice." It'll sound like a gentle nasal vowel.
- **c** Bring back your favorite image and smell it again, this time allowing the aroma into your mouth and throat as well. If you're working without smell, try to make the pool of cool air expand in your nose and back of your mouth and throat.
- **d** On the next exhale, gently allow some voice to move through this space. Did the sound change?
- **e** Now try breathing just through your mouth. Feel the cool air moving through your mouth and throat.
- **f** On your next exhale send voice through that space.
- **g** Breathe in your image through your mouth, allowing the pool of cool air to expand.
- **h** On your next exhale send voice through that space. Did the sound change? Mine gets a bit "yawny."

3 Expanding the laryngopharynx (sternohyoid, sternothyroid, thyrohyoid, omohyoid):
- **a** Place your hand on your larynx to feel for movement.
- **b** Lower your larynx and speak. Listen to the quality of your voice.

i **Pro Tip:** The larynx lowers when we yawn! Pretend to yawn to start that movement, then try it without yawning.

   ii If you're still having trouble moving your larynx, try imitating the Cowardly Lion, Darth Vader, or the Jolly Green Giant. You'll likely depress your larynx when you do so!

   c Try changing the pitch with a lowered larynx and feel what that's like.

4 Constricting the oropharynx and nasopharynx:

   a Send voice through your "yawny" open pharynx.

   b Swallow and try to feel the shape of the pharynx as it closes to move the saliva down the esophagus.

   c Try to hold that closed feeling as you send voice through it.

   i Can you keep your tongue a bit more relaxed?

   ii What does this sound like? To me, I think of this as a froggy or muppety sound.

5 Constricting the laryngopharynx (suprahyoid muscles: digastric, stylohyoid, geniohyoid, mylohyoid):

   a Place your hand on your larynx to feel for movement.

   b Raise your larynx and speak. It may feel like raising the tongue root. If you're having trouble moving your larynx up, try imitating the Wicked Witch of the West, Waluigi, or the Aflac Duck.

   c Try changing the pitch with a raised larynx and feel what that's like.

6 Happy medium:

   a Go back and forth between the "yawny" and "froggy" sounds—the sounds of the expanded and constricted pharynx.

   b Find the shape that feels like a happy medium, where the muscles can be open and relaxed. Try speaking while feeling that shape.

THE WORK OF AWARENESS

Well done! Now that you've explored each of those movements, go back and take note of what was easy for you and what you need more practice doing. Make sure to hit your weaker areas a few times per week in your daily practice. I still need to work on spreading my tongue and cupping before I can quickly and easily use these movements on purpose. So I add them to my daily routine and practice while I'm cooking or reading.

Activate

This is a hodgepodge of articulation exercises from every teacher and colleague I've ever had or read about. Even the ones I think I've invented are just mash-ups of the material I learned along the way. I'll name a few of my influences here as a way of summoning their energies to help us on the journey: Nancy Houfek, Catherine Fitzmaurice, Dudley Knight, Andrea Caban, Phil Thompson, Beth McGuire, Jane Guyer Fujita, Edith Skinner, Tim Monich, Lilene Mansell, Diego Daniel Pardo, Barbara Adrian, Arthur Lessac, Andrew Wade, Cicely Berry, Kristin Linklater. Their combined work makes up quite a bit of my speech identity. It was easy for me to identify myself in their work because their social locations are similar to my own. I say this because the texts I'll share at the end of this section are all written for my dialect. Their usefulness is not because of that dialect, but rather because of the dexterity they require. As you encounter texts that both require extra dexterity and feel like they're a closer match to your identity than Gilbert and Sullivan, swap them in! This will make your practice more fun and more personal. In the meantime, you can go through this series as an articulation workout, or pick and choose your sticky wickets to add to your daily practice.

Tongue-ups

This group of exercises is a bridge between the curling exercise we used to isolate the tongue and the articulation exercises we'll use to activate it. They're like target practice for your tongue, so be sure that your jaw is not doing the work. You can work the whole tongue, or focus on the spots you need for your speech goals.

1. Scratch the whole surface of the tongue along the top teeth to wake it up and prime it for action.
2. Tongue tip to the alveolar ridge:
   a. Curl the tip of your tongue to the sharp edge of the incisors.
   b. Scratch the tip of your tongue there for five seconds to wake it up.
   c. Now curl the tip of your tongue straight up into the alveolar ridge, then release it back down behind the bottom front teeth.
   d. Press and release ten times.
   e. Invent some sounds as you press and release.
3. Blade of the tongue to the alveolar ridge:
   a. Scratch the blade of your tongue (the spot behind the tip) on the sharp edge of the incisors for five seconds to wake it up.
   b. Curl the blade of your tongue to the alveolar ridge and then release it back down behind the bottom front teeth.
   c. Press and release ten times.
   d. Invent some sounds as you press and release.
4. Middle body of the tongue to the palate:
   a. Imagine there's peanut butter (or cold molasses, for our friends with allergies) stuck to the roof of your mouth.
   b. Keep the tip of your tongue touching your bottom front teeth and scratch the goo off of the roof of your mouth with the body of your tongue. This will wake up the middle of your tongue and the palate.
   c. Bring the middle of your tongue straight up to the palate and back down like an elevator.
   d. Press and release ten times.
   e. Invent some sounds while you press and release. These can get real fun!

5 Back body of the tongue:

   a Snort a couple of times with your mouth open to wake up the velum.

   b Touch the back of your tongue to your velum while keeping the tip of your tongue on your lower teeth.

   c Press and release ten times.

   d You know the drill. Make some noises.

Rhythmic articulation

This exercise is like ogres, onions, and parfait. It's layered! First and foremost, you'll be working your articulators with specific sounds. Second, you'll be working with a few of the common rhythm patterns of English, which will become more of a focus when and if you start working on poetry. We'll unpack the rhythmic aspect of this exercise in the prosody chapter (Chapter 7). For now, read across each row and back with the specified rhythm patterns. Try applying a bit more pressure with your articulators than you're used to, without gripping the jaw, and then build up speed as you get more and more comfortable.

1 Trochee—the rhythm like that in the word "taco." It has two syllables, with **stress** or emphasis, on the first syllable.

PApa   BAba   TAta   DAda   NAna   LAla   KAka   GAga

2 Anapest—the rhythm of the word "contradict" or the phrase "in the pool." It has three syllables, with stress on the third.

papaPAH   babaBAH   tataTAH   dadaDAH

nanaNAH   lalaLAH   kakaKAH   gagaGAH

3 Dactyl—the rhythm in the word "poetry." It has three syllables, with stress on the first. Let's make this more interesting! Can you articulate the "K" and "G" sounds as fast as the "T" and "D" sounds?

PIHpihpih PIHpihpih PIHpihpih PAH

BIHbihbih BIHbihbih BIHbihbih BAH

TIHtihtih TIHtihtih TIHtihtih TAH

DIHdihdih DIHdihdih DIHdihdih DAH

NIHnihnih NIHnihnih NIHnihnih NAH

LIHlihlih LIHlihlih LIHlihlih LAH

KIHkihkih KIHkihkih KIHkihkih KAH

GIHgihgih GIHgihgih GIHgihgih GAH

4 **Iamb**—the rhythm of the word "about" or the exclamation "It burns!" It has two syllables, with stress on the second. In this exercise, the vowels of the stressed syllables follow an AH, EY (like "hey"), EE, OH, OO pattern. Make sure we hear the final consonant sound!

pa**Pop** pa**Pape** pa**Peep** pa**Pope** pa**Poop**
ba**Bob** ba**Babe** ba**Beeb** ba**Bobe** ba**Boob**
ta**Tot** ta**Tate** ta**Teet** ta**Tote** ta**Toot**
da**Dod** da**Dade** da**Deed** da**Dode** da**Dood**
na**Non** na**Nane** na**Neen** na**KNown** na**Noon**
la**Lol** la**Lale** la**Leel** la**Lole** la**Lool**
ka**Kok** ka**Cake** ka**Keek** ka**Koke** ka**Kook**
ga**Gog** ga**Gage** ga**Geeg** ga**Goge** ga**Goog**

Tongue twisters

Bring that new consonant energy to words. Remember the rules of comedy: louder, faster, funnier!

1. paper poppy (four times), baby bubble (four times), paper poppy baby bubble (four times).
2. Topeka (four times), bodega (four times), Topeka bodega (four times).
3. mommola (four times), poppola (four times), mommola poppola (four times) (feel how you use your lips differently for "M" and "P").
4. The Leith police dismisseth us and that sufficeth us.
5. You know New York. You need New York. You know you need unique New York.
6. Peter Piper, the pickled pepper picker, picked a peck of pickled peppers.

THE WORK OF AWARENESS

A peck of pickled peppers did Peter Piper, the pickled pepper picker, pick.
Now, if Peter Piper, the pickled pepper picker, picked a peck of pickled peppers,
Where is the peck of pickled peppers that Peter Piper, the pickled pepper picker, picked?

Connect to text

The following texts are difficult, especially when performed quickly, but they're not necessarily tongue twisters. They have a bit more meaning behind them. Perform the following texts with as much dexterity as the tongue twisters above, but let your mind be focused on the meaning instead of the exercise. How do the difficult sounds help tell the story?

1   "Oh! Here's a To-Do," *Merrie England*, by Edward German and Basil Hood
    O, here's a to-do to die today at a minute-or-two to two;
    A thing distinctly hard to say, but harder still to do;
    For they'll beat a tattoo at two-to-two,
    A ratta-tat-tat tattoo for you,
    And the dragon will come when it hears the drum
    At a minute-or-two to two today, at a minute-or-two to two.

2   "Major General's Song," *Pirates of Penzance*, by W. S. Gilbert and Arthur Sullivan
    I am the very model of a modern major general,
    I've information vegetable, animal, and mineral,
    I know the kings of England, and I quote the fights historical,
    From Marathon to Waterloo, in order categorical;
    I'm very well acquainted, too, with matters mathematical,
    I understand equations, both the simple and quadratical,
    About binomial theorem I'm teeming with a lot o' news,
    With many cheerful facts about the square of the hypotenuse.

3   "The Drunkard," traditional elocution rhyme, author unknown
    Amidst the mists and coldest frosts,
    With stoutest wrists and loudest boasts,
    He thrusts his fists against the posts,
    And still insists he sees the ghosts.

4 "Ode," by Arthur O'Shaughnessy
We are the music makers,
And we are the dreamers of dreams,
Wandering by lone sea-breakers,
And sitting by desolate streams;—
World-losers and world-forsakers,
On whom the pale moon gleams:
Yet we are the movers and shakers
Of the world for ever, it seems.

6
THE SHAPE OF YOUR SOUND

In the previous chapter, we explored some of the distinct ways that you can use your anatomy as you move through your thoughts. When you have the impulse to speak, you turn your thoughts into speech by performing a dance between your articulators in the specific style of your idiolect. As you practice the individual dance steps, you're becoming aware of which moves are a natural part of your repertoire and which feel outside the bounds of your habits. Those boundaries are the actual shape of you—of your **vocal tract**, to be precise.

The shape of the vocal tract changes the sound that comes out of a speaker in the same way that the shape of a musical instrument changes the quality of the notes that come out of it. Some of that shape is due to genetics. No two people will have the same physical structure, so no two voices can be identical. The other aspect of that shape is **vocal tract posture**—the habitual usage of the muscles that change how breath and vibration move through the vocal tract. Like a muscle in your arm that you work out in order to change its shape, the muscles of the vocal tract get built up by the repeated speech habits of your idiolect into specific shapes. Those shapes—your boundaries—make it easier for the habitual sounds to be articulated while making other sounds more work.

Think back to the isolation exercises you've been working on. Table 3 is a list of some of the ways that the movements you found can be transformed into vocal tract posture. These movements are usually on a spectrum of activation. There are accents with somewhat rounded lips and accents with very rounded lips. In the table, each row shows which region in the vocal tract we're exploring, what detail we're describing, and the spectrum of possibilities for that detail.

TABLE 3 *Vocal Tract Posture*

Place	Characteristic	Spectrum of possibilities			
Jaw	height	more closed	neutral	more open	
	placement	protruded	neutral	Retracted	
	activity	more active	neutral	more relaxed	
Lips	shape	rounded	relaxed	Spread	
	rounding style	pursed	mixed	Trumpeted	
	height	raised	relaxed	Lowered	
	activity	more active	neutral	more relaxed	
Cheeks	zygomaticus	raised	Relaxed		
	buccinator	braced	Relaxed		
Tongue	thickness	bunched	neutral	Spread	
	shape	more curled	more bunched	arched backward	
	area of tip articulation	bottom tip	tip	top tip	Blade
Velum	height	raised (no nasality)	neutral (mixed)	lowered (nasal)	
Root	placement	advanced	neutral	Retracted	
Pharynx	constriction	widened	neutral	narrowed	
Larynx	height	lowered	neutral	raised	
Glottis	plosives	present	not present		
	register	whispered	creaky	breathy	modal

Exercise: Vocal tract posture

Go through the chart and speak some text while activating each muscle isolation on the different levels of the spectrum. Keep it loose! If it feels like you can't speak because you're holding the vocal tract posture too strongly, let it relax a little bit, so your articulators can dance around the general shape. Have fun. This is one of my favorite activities and it's super useful if you need a cartoon voice on the fly.

Play: Character interviews

Now that you've explored the range of possibilities for vocal tract posture individually, it's time to have fun with it. In this exercise you're going to mix and match vocal tract posture details to create fun characters. Do this with a partner or a group, or you can film yourself. It's a hoot and it may be my favorite exercise in the book. (But don't tell the others.)

1. Choose a vocal tract posture detail and where on its spectrum you want to perform it.

2. Walk around the room and practice speaking as "easily" as possible with this single detail in place. This is your new character.

3. Choose a name for this character and begin to introduce yourself to the other folks in the room—either real or imaginary. Have a conversation if you can. If there's nobody there, give a speech about why you should be elected class treasurer.

4. Choose a second detail and try to keep both of them active, speaking as "easily" as possible. This is a new character.

5. Pick a new name for your second character and begin introducing yourself. If you have nobody to talk to, give a little speech about your favorite TV show or book.

6. Choose a third vocal tract posture detail and try to keep all of them active. This is a third character.

7. Pick a new name for your third character and begin introducing yourself or give a little speech about a topic close to your character's heart.

8. If you're working in a group, after all the third introductions have been made, a volunteer can be interviewed by the crowd while everyone keeps their vocal tract posture attributes in place. "What's your name?" "What's your favorite candy?" etc. After the volunteer has answered a few questions, the interviewers can guess which three vocal tract posture details the character is using. If you're working alone, practice your character's award acceptance speech.

Idiolectsploration: Vocal tract posture

As you explored changing your vocal tract posture, you may have noticed that some movements were easy and some took more work or concentration to hold on to. You can use that kind of information to find your own vocal tract posture. Is a detail easy because it's close to how you use your vocal tract, or is it easy because it's the opposite extreme? Do certain details sound or feel familiar? Go through Table 3 again, this time thinking about your own vocal tract posture. Use Table 4 to write notes and then draw a picture describing each region. The picture can be as specific or as abstract as you like. Don't worry about being perfect right now. As you go through the exercises in this book, you might learn more and more about your vocal tract posture and can always come back here and edit.

TABLE 4 *Vocal Tract Posture of My Idiolect*

Articulator	Notes	Picture
Lips		
Cheeks		
Jaw		
Tongue		
Velum		
Tongue root		
Pharynx		
Larynx		
Glottis		

7
YOUR OWN KIND OF MUSIC

Let's pause for a moment and take stock of all the work you've done so far. You've learned how to mine text for the twists and turns of the images. You've explored your own personal images and what they mean to you. You then practiced techniques to make a writer's language choices feel as personal and active as the images that are part of your idiolect. You then became aware of your speech anatomy and the movements that are possible to create speech. You took that awareness and applied it to the shape of your vocal tract and how that affects your idiolect. This chapter is a combination of all these concepts and techniques.

Now that we've analyzed the sense of the language and what it means to you, and the ways we can use the anatomy to change our sound, we can explore the tools we use to convey meaning, context, and intention while speaking. Take the sentence "My dog likes running in the front yard." Say it out loud. Now try changing which word is the most important. "My dog likes running in the front YARD." "My dog LIKES running in the front yard." "My dog likes running in the FRONT yard." "MY dog likes running in the front yard." What did you change in order to make different words the most important? How did changing the important words also change the intention of that thought? Your answer likely has something to do with **prosody**—the rhythm, pitch, pace, and volume of speech. Let's explore these concepts in a way that we're used to dealing with them—through music!

Play: Dancing to the music

1 Listen to the song "Oye Como Va," by Tito Puente. Let your body move in reaction to the *rhythm*. Try to disregard the pitch completely and just move to the rhythm.

2 Now listen to "Gran Varon" by Willie Colón. Let your body move in reaction to just the *pace*, or speed, of the music. Don't confuse pace and rhythm! Rhythm is the relative length of notes and how they rest in relationship to one another. Speed is how fast or slow you would clap to keep time.

3 Listen to the song "Over the Rainbow," from *The Wizard of Oz*. Move your body in reaction to the *pitch* of Judy Garland's voice. Do your best to disregard the rhythm as much as you can.

4 Listen to "Total Eclipse of the Heart," by Bonnie Tyler. Move your body in reaction to just the *volume* of the music.

Speech rhythm is similar to rhythm in music. It's the relative length of syllables and the pauses in between them. Speech rhythms can be even and measured or uneven and more jagged feeling. Rhythm includes lengthening some words and shortening others. There's usually a pattern to these types of rhythms, and the patterns will stay the same even as the pace of speech changes. When the pace of a thought increases, you will move between operative words faster. You'll actually speak more operative words per minute. Pitch is the same in music and speech, with highs and lows depending on how important each word is. I also like to listen for *how* the pitch moves. Does it slide from pitch to pitch or does it jump from one pitch to the next? Do operative words spike in pitch or do they dip? Last, there's speech volume, which might be changed to make a point, to insert yourself into a conversation, to tell a secret, and so on. We combine all these factors to reveal to our audience the meaning and intention behind the words we're saying.

Play: Dancing to your own music

I'd like you to dance again, but this time you'll use the recording of your personal story as your music. Let your body move in reaction to each of the components of prosody and write down some observations. If it's hard to tell how your voice is moving, write down observations about your body movement instead.

1. Rhythm: describe your speech rhythm generally. Is there a lot of rhythm change, or is it relatively regular? Does the rhythm feel jagged or smooth? When do you lengthen words and when do you shorten them?
2. Pace: describe the speed of your speech. Does the speed change or does it always stay consistent?
3. Pitch: describe the pitch generally. Is there a lot of pitch movement or a little? When the pitch moves, does it slide or jump?
4. Volume: does your volume change during your story? Does it change quickly or gradually?

Idiolectsploration: Prosody

Listen to the recording of your personal story while paying attention to each of the following prompts. You'll listen to your story a total of seven times for this exploration. Observe how you're using prosody to bring meaning and context to the words. You can pause your story and write down any notes if you hear something interesting about your rhythm, speed, pitch, or volume. Dance along if you need to in order to be as specific as you can. Observe how you use prosody to accomplish the following:

1. Let the listener know where each thought starts and ends.
2. Change direction in the thought. What does your prosody do around where the comma would go if your speech were written?
3. Make a noun or a verb important. Are there levels of importance?
4. Compare one thing to another thing.
5. Make any corrections or addendums to your thoughts.
6. Create a setup and a payoff.
7. De-emphasize the function words that would be crossed out.

The way you use prosody to match your words to your intentions is a deeply ingrained aspect of your accent. Like everything about your speech, the observations you made about your musicality have their roots in every person or community who has been important to you up to this point in your life. Still, prosody is one aspect of a person's accent that can drastically change in different situations. Changing one's accent in different situations is called **code-switching**, and it is a normal part of life. Think about some of the code-switching you might do when talking to friends, parents, grandparents, babies, pets, customers, authority figures, etc. If you code-switch, a character could too.

Idiolectsploration: Prosody of reading

Listen to your recording of *Stella Starchild*. Observe if your prosody is different from your personal story at all.

    Chances are, something changed about your prosody when you read as opposed to when you told your personal story extemporaneously. This kind of code-switching can be useful to help the listener understand the story when you can't use extra words to clarify. Sometimes, however, other habits creep in when we read or memorize text that no longer fit the language or circumstances of the story. These extraneous habits can be so strong that the meaning can become lost. So, the same way we broke the language down in order to make more mindful choices, let's break down some of ways we use prosody.

Syllables

I'm guessing you already know roughly what a syllable is. I describe a **syllable** as a pulse of sound energy. In their book *Practical English Phonetics and Phonology*, Beverley Collins, Inger M. Mees, and Paul Carley define a syllable as "a linguistic unit larger than a phoneme and smaller than the word, usually containing a vowel as its nucleus."[1] There's a lot to unpack in that definition because syllables are treated differently in different languages. For our purposes, we can go back to our music analogy and say that syllables are the beats of a word. "Um" takes one beat, as do "sum," "strum," and "strums." I'll mention here that "beat" is not a perfect definition. In languages like Japanese, the

---

[1] Collins, Mees, and Carley, *Practical English Phonetics and Phonology*.

length of each syllable is important, so a syllable can have two beats, or morae, and it will mean something different than the same syllable with one mora. But again, for English purposes, let's just think "beat" or "pulse."

Exercise: Counting syllables

How many syllables do you hear in the following samples? If you're not sure, try clapping the word instead of speaking it. How many claps did you perform? Here's another option if clapping doesn't work out. You can place your hand on your chin and overexaggerate your enunciation of each word like you're trying to get someone to read your lips. The number of times your chin moves will be the number of syllables.

schools   timely   expressive   mitochondria   coronary

In my accent, the words shown have one, two, three, five, and four syllables, in that order. That's not a definitive answer, however, because different accents will pronounce different words differently. I'm hoping there are some folks reading this who would pronounce "coronary" as "coron'ry," with three syllables. Both of these pronunciations are correct for the accents in which they occur, so I won't call one better than the other. Let's look at the component parts of a syllable, which stay the same from accent to accent.

Here, we're going to break down how individual speech sounds, or **phonemes,** make up a syllable. Say the one-syllable word, "tack." How many phonemes can you identify? I make 3: a "T" sound, an "AA" sound, and a "K" sound at the end. Every syllable has what is called a **nucleus**, which is the most vowel-like of all of the syllable's sounds. Sing something to yourself. In each syllable you sing, the nucleus is the part that you hold out. If the nucleus has a consonant sound before it, the consonant is called the **syllable onset**. If there is a consonant after the nucleus, it's called the **syllable coda**. In "tack," the nucleus is the "AA" vowel. The syllable onset is the "T" and the syllable coda is the "K."

Exercise: Syllable structure

We'll go over vowels and consonants later on, but do your best to answer the following.

1 What is the nucleus of the syllable "bet"?
2 Which consonant is the syllable onset for the syllable "bet"?
3 Which consonant is the syllable coda for the syllable "bet"?
4 Some words will have a group of consonants, or a **consonant cluster**, in the onset or coda of a syllable. Which consonant(s) is (are) the syllable onset for the word "school"? (Hint: think sounds, not spelling. Say the word. What sounds do you hear before "OO"?)

Word stress

In English, words with multiple syllables will have one or more that stand out from the rest. This is called **word stress**. I listen for the pitch of the syllables to hear the word stress. The syllable with the most extreme pitch change is called **primary stress**. In my accent, that would normally be the highest pitch of the word. The second-most extreme pitch change is called **secondary stress**. The syllables around the stressed syllables that aren't emphasized are **unstressed** syllables. The International Phonetic Alphabet marks stress before the syllable in question. Primary stress is marked with / ' / before the syllable (e.g., 'ca.lling) and secondary stress is marked with / ˌ / before the syllable (e.g., 'flab.berˌgas.ted). Unstressed syllables are often left unmarked, but to discuss where syllables start and stop, we can separate them with a period (e.g., 'fla.bberˌga.sted). Excuse my use of letters instead of the IPA symbols for the sounds. We'll get there! We're halfway between how a dictionary will show the word and how a linguist might.

Exercise: Word stress

Record yourself saying the following list of words, then dance the pitch of these words the way you danced to the pitch of "Over the Rainbow." Mark the primary, secondary, and unstressed syllables for each. Keep this recording for later.

Key:

primary stress / ' /   secondary stress / ˌ /   unstressed /. /
lefty   asymmetrical   garage   bicentennial   motherly   uncommon

Thought stress

Now that we've explored how stress works inside a single word, we can talk about how it works in a thought. **Thought stress** is the way we use prosody to make words or phrases stand out in a sentence and to make our point. This is the movement of the thoughts that we've been exploring. We create importance through contrast. Each thought has a basic pitch range of stressed and unstressed syllables and moves from there when contrast is needed. When a word is important to the thought, the speaker will change the pitch and possibly the length of its stressed syllable to contrast that word from the rest of the thought. This word has become an operative word. If the operative word is more than one syllable, the unstressed syllables return to the basic pitch range. As an example, think back to the sentence "My dog likes running in the front yard." If you were to try "My dog likes RUNNING in the front yard," even though "running" is two syllables, in order to pluck this word out from the thought, you'd only emphasize the pitch of the stressed syllable. I'm being intentionally vague here about how the pitch will change, because different accents of English will use different pitch variations. If you listen to accents from Cardiff, Mississippi, Detroit, London, Cape Town, Melbourne, Mumbai, etc., each will have their own way of using pitch to make a point. What's yours?

Idiolectsploration: The movement of thoughts

Listen to the recording you made of "Playing with sentence structures" (Chapter 1). Draw the movement of the pitch for each sentence. Are any patterns emerging? Do you tend to raise the pitch of the stressed syllables of important words, or lower them? If you're on a roll, listen to how you use operative words in your personal story and *Stella Starchild*.

Rhythm

You may have noticed in your personal story that entire phrases can be the "operative words." Even the term "operative words" is a phrase! In that case, the pitches of the stressed syllables of each important word move away from the main pitch. The unstressed syllables and interstitial function words can stay close to the main pitch range. The farther the pitch of the stressed syllable is from its surroundings, the more important it sounds. I see the pitch of each thought moving like telephone wire—peaking at each pole (operative syllables) and sagging in between.

Now, buckle up, because this next bit is magical. English, among other languages, is what's known as a **stress-timed** language, meaning there is roughly the same amount of time between all the operative syllables of a thought. Other languages, like Spanish or Cantonese, are **syllable-timed**, meaning each syllable takes roughly the same amount of time. Some languages, like Japanese, Slovak, and Ganda, are **mora-timed** languages, meaning each of the beats within syllables of a thought is roughly the same length as the others. In those languages you can have syllables of different lengths, but those lengths are predetermined. In English, however, we subconsciously lengthen some operative syllables and shorten the unstressed syllables and function words in between them so that the important images in a thought are laid out roughly evenly. To bring this back to my telephone pole analogy, some of the sagging wires will be many syllables long and others might have one or no syllables before the next pole, but there will be roughly the same amount of space between each operative word pole.

I've heard acting teachers wisely say, "Every word is important. Honor every word." I totally agree. The words in your text are like the parts of a car—each one is necessary to get where you're going safely and effectively. You can't drive, however, while putting as much attention on the axle as you do on the steering wheel, gas pedal, or brakes. You really should have your attention on the road and other drivers so you can respond to changes when needed. The function words in your text that are crossed out are like the axle of the thought. They are important insomuch as they create the structure and movement of the thought, but you won't put your attention on them every time you take a ride. If you give them too much attention, you'll lose the rhythm of the thought, and it will be unintelligible. Again, I hold that we create importance through contrast, so if everything is always even, we lose the point of the thought. It's why the quintessential robot voice lacks pitch and rhythm contrast, because it isn't conveying thoughts and the feelings behind them; it's conveying words in order. The robot voice lacks thought stress.

Exercise: Rhythmic articulation 2, syllable timing

Let's revisit the rhythmic articulation exercise (from "Exercise: Activate" in Chapter 5) and explore another layer—the use of unstressed syllables. We'll practice various speech rhythms by transforming word stress into practice syllables and then into small phrases all with the same rhythm pattern.

1. Iamb—short-long:
   a Read the following and notice the rhythm:
   about, about, about, about, about
   b Read the following with the same rhythm as "about":
   ~~tuh~~-tah, ~~tuh~~-tah, ~~tuh~~-tah, ~~tuh~~-tah, ~~tuh~~-tah
   c Add words:
   ~~I~~ got ~~the~~ wine ~~from~~ Jim ~~to~~ bring ~~to~~ Tom.

Remember, "~~to~~ Tom" should sound very similar to "~~tuh~~-tah," because function words are allowed to be shortened to what's called their weak form. In the weak form, they sound like "I got th'wine frm Jim t'bring t'Tom." Short-long, short-long, short-long, short-long, short-long.

2. Trochee—long-short:
   a Read the following and notice the rhythm:
   comma, comma, comma, comma, comma
   b Read the following with the same rhythm as "comma":
   tah-~~tuh~~, tah-~~tuh~~, tah-~~tuh~~, tah-~~tuh~~, tah-~~tuh~~
   c Add words, allowing the function words to be weak forms:
   Zach ~~and~~ Martha ate ~~a~~ lot ~~of~~ tacos.

3. Anapest—short-short-long:
   a Read the following and notice the rhythm:
   understand, understand, understand, understand, understand
   b Read the following with the same rhythm as "understand":
   ~~tuh-tuh~~-tah, ~~tuh-tuh~~-tah, ~~tuh-tuh~~-tah, ~~tuh-tuh~~-tah, ~~tuh-tuh~~-tah

    c Add words while allowing the function words to be weak forms:

        If we go to the store then I'd like to be home around eight.

4 Dactyl—long-short-short:

    a Read the following and notice the rhythm:

        formerly, formerly, formerly, formerly, formerly

    b Read the following with the same rhythm as "formerly":

        tah-tuh-tuh, tah-tuh-tuh, tah-tuh-tuh, tah-tuh-tuh, tah-tuh-tuh

    c Add words, allowing the function words to be weak forms:

        Billy and Martha were acting with Addie and Pamela.

5 Add your favorite consonants to the syllable onset to practice each rhythm:

    a Iamb ("about")
        tuh-tah, tuh-tah, tuh-tah, tuh-tah, tuh-tah
        duh-dah, duh-dah, duh-dah, duh-dah, duh-dah
        nuh-nah, nuh-nah, nuh-nah, nuh-nah, nuh-nah
        luh-lah, luh-lah, luh-lah, luh-lah, luh-lah
        shuh-shah, shuh-shah, shuh-shah, shuh-shah, shuh-shah
        (voiced like "the") thuh-thah, thuh-thah, thuh-thah, thuh-thah, thuh-thah
        wuh-wah, wuh-wah, wuh-wah, wuh-wah, wuh-wah
        fruh-frah, fruh-frah, fruh-frah, fruh-frah, fruh-frah

    b Trochee ("comma")
        tah-tuh, tah-tuh, tah-tuh, tah-tuh, tah-tuh
        dah-duh, dah-duh, dah-duh, dah-duh, dah-duh
        nah-nuh, nah-nuh, nah-nuh, nah-nuh, nah-nuh
        lah-luh, lah-luh, lah-luh, lah-luh, lah-luh
        shah-shuh, shah-shuh, shah-shuh, shah-shuh, shah-shuh
        thah-thuh, thah-thuh, thah-thuh, thah-thuh, thah-thuh
        wah-wuh, wah-wuh, wah-wuh, wah-wuh, wah-wuh
        frah-fruh, frah-fruh, frah-fruh, frah-fruh, frah-fruh

    c Anapest ("understand")
        tuh-tuh-tah, tuh-tuh-tah, tuh-tuh-tah, tuh-tuh-tah, tuh-tuh-tah
        duh-duh-dah, duh-duh-dah, duh-duh-dah, duh-duh-dah, duh-duh-dah

nuh-nuh-nah, nuh-nuh-nah, nuh-nuh-nah, nuh-nuh-nah, nuh-nuh-nah
luh-luh-lah, luh-luh-lah, luh-luh-lah, luh-luh-lah, luh-luh-lah
shuh-shuh-shah, shuh-shuh-shah, shuh-shuh-shah, shuh-shuh-shah, shuh-shuh-shah
thuh-thuh-thah, thuh-thuh-thah, thuh-thuh-thah, thuh-thuh-thah, thuh-thuh-thah
wuh-wuh-wah, wuh-wuh-wah, wuh-wuh-wah, wuh-wuh-wah, wuh-wuh-wah
fruh-fruh-frah, fruh-fruh-frah, fruh-fruh-frah, fruh-fruh-frah, fruh-fruh-frah

d Dactyl ("formerly")

tah-tuh-tuh, tah-tuh-tuh, tah-tuh-tuh, tah-tuh-tuh, tah-tuh-tuh
dah-duh-duh, dah-duh-duh, dah-duh-duh, dah-duh-duh, dah-duh-duh
nah-nuh-nuh, nah-nuh-nuh, nah-nuh-nuh, nah-nuh-nuh, nah-nuh-nuh
lah-luh-luh, lah-luh-luh, lah-luh-luh, lah-luh-luh, lah-luh-luh
shah-shuh-shuh, shah-shuh-shuh, shah-shuh-shuh, shah-shuh-shuh, shah-shuh-shuh
thah-thuh-thuh, thah-thuh-thuh, thah-thuh-thuh, thah-thuh-thuh, thah-thuh-thuh
wah-wuh-wuh, wah-wuh-wuh, wah-wuh-wuh, wah-wuh-wuh, wah-wuh-wuh
frah-fruh-fruh, frah-fruh-fruh, frah-fruh-fruh, frah-fruh-fruh, frah-fruh-fruh

Exercise: Rhythm and language analysis

Now that you're aware of these rhythms in isolation, you're ready to explore them in your text. In this exercise, you'll go through "The New Colossus" (see page 33) line by line to discover the rhythm of the language. Start with the first line and complete all the following prompts, then move on to the second line. Once you get the hang of it, feel free to move thought by thought.

1 Look at the words you haven't crossed off. These will be your operative words and phrases.

2 If any of these operative words or phrases are more than one syllable, make a note of where the stressed and unstressed syllables are.

   a You likely now have found at least one of the rhythms that we practiced in the previous exercise. Speak this word or phrase with that rhythm in mind.

   b For example, you might practice speaking "brazen giant" as two trochees in a row.

3 Notice the words that are crossed out. These are unstressed syllables. How might they change how you feel each rhythm?

   a I now might feel "~~the~~ brazen giant" as two iambs plus an unstressed syllable after.

   b I can expand this exploration to include the entire noun phrase. "The brazen giant of Greek fame," could be felt as iamb, iamb, short-short, long-long. In this version, we've discovered two more rhythm patterns: the **pyrrhic**, two unstressed syllables in succession, and the **spondee**, two stressed syllables in succession.

4 Speak the whole line, moving seamlessly through the stressed and unstressed syllables.

5 When you've finished a whole thought, put the lines together and speak the entire thought with your attention on the rhythms.

   a What would it feel like to lengthen the stressed syllables a little bit more?

   b What would it feel like to shorten the unstressed syllables even more?

   c Let your imagination into the game by folding in imaginary circumstances. How can you lengthen certain important syllables or words to get what your character needs?

Pitch

You may have noticed in that last exercise that if you lengthen a syllable without also moving the pitch, it sounds off. That's because rhythm and pitch work together as we move through the operative words and phrases of a thought. These two features help us reveal what's behind the words we're saying. How many times in your life have you said a perfectly innocent sentence, but the "tone of your voice" has betrayed some other meaning or intention? That's how powerful a tool pitch can be. Sometimes, however, actors can get stuck speaking a repetitive pitch pattern that doesn't reveal anything about their point of view. This often happens because they've memorized the line with that pitch pattern and then they think the line can only be delivered in that way. Getting out of these "line readings" can be tough. The first step is learning to control your pitch on purpose.

Exercise: Pitch

In this exercise you will practice changing your pitch on purpose by moving through your vocal range.

1. Count from one to ten while sliding up your comfortable pitch range on one breath. One should be the lowest note you can comfortably speak and ten should be as high you as you can comfortably speak. Pay attention to about where the pitch of each number falls in your pitch range.

2. Count from ten back down to one on one breath while sliding down your comfortable pitch range. Pay attention to about where the pitch of each number falls in your voice. Each number should land somewhere near where it was while you were counting up, but it won't be exact.

3. Speak the following sequence while trying to match the numbers to around where they were in your pitch range in the first two steps.

a	1		**i**	8
b	1, 2, 1		**j**	8, 7, 8
c	1, 3, 1		**k**	8, 6, 8
d	1, 4, 1		**l**	8, 5, 8
e	1, 5, 1		**m**	8, 4, 8
f	1, 6, 1		**n**	8, 3, 8
g	1, 7, 1		**o**	8, 2, 8
h	1, 8, 1		**p**	8, 1, 8

4 If it sounds as if you're singing instead of speaking, don't hold the note steadily; let it fall off toward the bottom of your voice. To put it more simply: speak, don't sing.

5 If you notice yourself yelling or getting quieter, you might have switched to changing your volume instead of your pitch. Try to isolate the pitch while speaking with a steady volume.

6 Repeat steps 1 and 2, then perform the following sequence.

a	5		**g**	5
b	5, 6, 5		**h**	5, 4, 5
c	5, 7, 5		**i**	5, 3, 5
d	5, 8, 5		**j**	5, 2, 5
e	5, 9, 5		**k**	5, 1, 5
f	5, 10, 5			

7 Repeat steps 3 and 6 while focusing on how the moving number sounds compared to the base pitch.

Using the middle of your range as your base pitch allows you the freedom to move up or down your pitch range to create word or thought stress. If your base pitch is always at 1 or if it's creaky, try letting your voice dance around your 3 range, then your 5 range. This will open up your options for expressivity. If it feels unnatural or forced when you speak text in this range, it's because it is at the moment. You probably have a larger pitch range when your emotional temperature rises, and right now you're reading a book about speech. But in the movie of your life, this bit will be an 1980s training montage and the writers will save your lines for the more important stuff. Similarly, writers often cut out the monotonous, unenergized parts of the characters' lives, so most of the lines you'll say will be from a more excited place.

Exercise: Pitch and language analysis

Let's apply your new pitch skills to the language analysis of "The New Colossus."

1. Read the poem aloud with your 3s or 5s as your basic pitch range.
2. Read it again, making sure that the words that are crossed out are all unstressed. The pitch of these words will stay in your basic pitch range. Be meticulous at first so you can really feel how unstressed they are.
3. Allow yourself to be more extreme with the pitch changes of the stressed syllables of the words and phrases that are not crossed out. It's okay for this to feel willy-nilly in this step.
4. Last, read it again with some circumstances built in.
   a. Who are you? Whom are you speaking to? What do you want them to do or feel? Why do you want that?
   b. When a word or phrase is important to your point, change the pitch of the stressed syllables of that word or phrase to make the person you're talking to understand how important it is. It's not enough that you know how you feel about the phrase; you need to make the person you're speaking to feel the phrase. To quote my colleague Walton Wilson, "Change with the changes."
   c. Start in your 5 range and lift off.

Pace

Have you ever seen an actor get overcome with nerves and start speaking a mile a minute? Or perhaps you noticed an actor slowly crawl through their lines in what is supposed to be an emergency situation.

The speed of speech is an important tool that helps an actor meet the given circumstances of the scene, but it's often overlooked or taken for granted. Speed, like pitch, is a prosody tool that we can control. We can choose to speed up or slow down as we navigate the moment-to-moment work of the scene. I learned the exercises in this section from my colleague Eliza Simpson. They'll bring awareness to the speed of your speech to help your pace become a choice instead of something that just happens.

Exercise: Pace and syllable timing

In this exercise, we're going to use a metronome. You can find free and easy-to-use metronomes online. It doesn't have to be fancy, but be sure that you can control the number of beats per minute (bpm).

1. Count from one to five at any speed: one, two, three, four, five.
2. Set your metronome to 60 bpm and listen to the speed of the clicks.
3. Count from one to five at the speed of the metronome, so each number is spoken at the same time as a click.
4. Set your metronome to 45 bpm and repeat.
5. Set your metronome to 90 bpm and repeat.

That exercise may have felt simple, but it's a clear way to really feel speech speeding up and slowing down. The numbers are acting as operative words and they're spoken with about the same amount of time between one and the next. Now we're going to add some syllables between the operative words to feel how we can change the speed of stressed and unstressed syllables. Because English is stress-timed, each number will still land on the click of the metronome, and the unstressed syllables will fit themselves in between clicks.

1. Count from one to five at any speed, with a syllable before each number to create iambs: a-one-a-two-a-three-a-four-a-five.
2. Set your metronome to 60 bpm and listen to the speed of the clicks.

3 Count from one to five at the speed of the metronome, so each number is spoken at the same time as a click with the added syllables preceding: a-one-a-two-a-three-a-four-a-five.

4 Set your metronome to 45 bpm and repeat: a-one-a-two-a-three-a-four-a-five.

5 Set your metronome to 90 bpm and repeat: a-one-a-two-a-three-a-four-a-five.

6 Count from one to five at any speed with two syllables before each number to create anapests: and-a-one-and-a-two-and-a-three-and-a-four-and-a-five.

7 Set your metronome to 60 bpm and listen to the speed of the clicks.

8 Count from one to five at the speed of the metronome, so each number is spoken at the same time as a click, with the added syllables preceding: and-a-one-and-a-two-and-a-three-and-a-four-and-a-five.

9 Set your metronome to 45 bpm and repeat: and-a-one-and-a-two-and-a-three-and-a-four-and-a-five.

10 Set your metronome to 90 bpm and repeat: and-a-one-and-a-two-and-a-three-and-a-four-and-a-five.

11 Repeat this exercise with trochees and dactyls: one-a-two-a-three-a-four-a-five-a and one-and-a-two-and-a-three-and-a-four-and-a-five-and-a.

12 Add words! Speak the sentences from the rhythm section at different speeds, putting the operative words on the clicks.

a I got the wine from Jim to bring to Tom.

b Zach and Martha ate a lot of tacos.

c If we go to the store then I'd like to be home around eight.

d Billy and Martha were acting with Addie and Pamela.

13 Real-life speech isn't quite as evenly spaced as speaking to a metronome, so can you speed up and slow down without the metronome?

14 Try it with "The New Colossus"!

    a Read the whole poem at different speeds.

    b You can also play with changing the speed of different sections to match the intention. If you don't know where to begin with those choices, start by changing your speed for the sections in quotes.

Volume

Volume is another feature of prosody that sometimes feels beyond an actor's control, but the ability to choose when to raise or lower your volume will help you meet the given circumstances of the scene. Maybe two characters are meeting in secret, or the town crier needs to get a room's attention. Perhaps the town crier needs to secretly warn someone of impending danger in between cries! There will be a more in-depth look into how breath, muscles, and bones turn into volume in a healthy way elsewhere in the series, but let's practice changing our volume on purpose to bring intention to the text.

Exercise: Changing volume

1 Count from one to five, then from five to one, with one being as quiet as you can comfortably speak and five being as loud as you can comfortably speak. Try to remember the volume of each number to repeat it later.

2 Repeat step 1, but keep your pitch consistent. You don't need to raise your pitch to increase your volume.

3 Repeat step 1 one more time, making sure that you're fully phonating the whole time. Try not to let the voice get breathy as it gets quiet. Full phonation can be just as quiet.

    a Speak the following patterns while changing your volume to match each number.

b	1	**g**	5
c	1, 2, 1	**h**	5, 4, 5,
d	1, 3, 1	**i**	5, 3, 5
e	1, 4, 1	**j**	5, 2, 5
f	1, 5, 1	**k**	5, 1, 5

4. Speak the "The New Colossus" with each line at a different volume. Let it be willy-nilly.
5. Speak the "The New Colossus" while changing your volume with each thought.
6. Speak the "The New Colossus" while changing your volume at each punctuation mark.

Now that you've had an experience of prosody, you can use these tools on purpose to bring meaning to your text. I highly recommend revisiting the word soaking exercise (see "Play: Word soaking" in Chapter 3). Rhythm, pitch, pace, and volume are the ways we give voice to that kind of personalization and specificity. If something changes inside you—if you have an impulse—the audience won't know unless you change something about how you're speaking. It's not enough to know what you're saying and why. That's the homework. The real art-making happens when you're able to stand on that foundation of analysis while responding to what's really happening to you as it happens. If something onstage catches your eye in a new way, is that good for you and your character or bad for you and your character? How good or bad is it? How is your next thought a response to that change? How do you reveal that response by using a change of rhythm, pitch, pace, or volume? Language analysis stays the same for the most part. It's figuring out the sense of the words that the playwright has given you. Prosody is where we have the most choice. It's how we make the performance our own. It's not enough to say the words in the right order in a way that can be understood. You get to make the audience feel—the way that music makes us feel. Speak the poem one more time. Know whom you're speaking to and why you're saying these words to them. Then make them feel it with the prosody.

Anything you do, feel, think, or say in this moment is happening to the character. Let it change you. Try to change whomever you're speaking to.

[1]IPA Chart. Available under a Creative Commons Attribution-Sharealike 3.0 Unported License. http://www.internationalphoneticassociation.org/content/ipa-chart. Copyright © 2018 International Phonetic Association.

8
RIVER OF SOUNDS

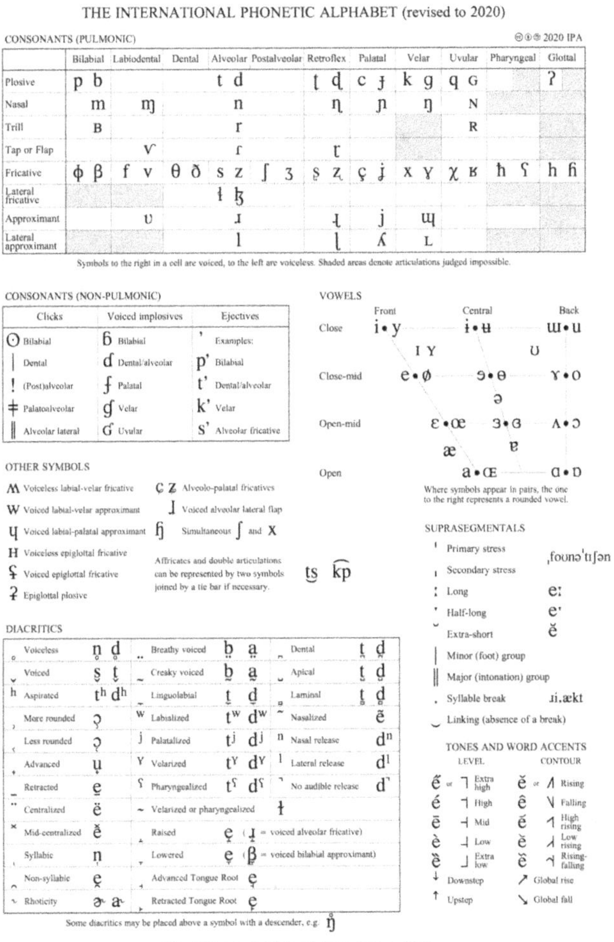

FIGURE 5 IPA chart.[1]

Phonology is the study of individual speech sounds, or phonemes, and how they behave in a language. It can be difficult to wrap your mind around the science of it at first, but it's something that's working in every speaker whether they notice it or not. Phonology also holds clues about who your people are and where they came from. The way that I pronounce the "L" in my full name, Ronald, comes directly from the fact that my grandparents lived in Yonkers, New York, with their young family. Even though I came of age in a different dialect region altogether, my accent features a sound clue to my family history. This idea affects an actor in a number of ways. When you use a sound or a pronunciation that is a specific part of your idiolect, you're drawing on the way your communities use sounds to get what they want. Depending on the situation or the person you're talking to, you might create a sound slightly differently to match the feeling you're trying to get across. Because the language is coming from you, it might be somewhat subconscious. You can have that same freedom to choose from your arsenal of sounds as an actor based on how you personalize the images of the text and the needs of the character. Think of the imaginative possibility of fully dropping yourself at this level of specificity into the world of the characters you play.

    This book can also be used as a jumping-off point for accent work that lets you find the idiolect of a character whose accent is different from your own. Or the reverse—you may have sounds in your accent phonology that are specific to a time or place that a director feels pulls the audience out of the imaginary circumstances of the performance. Understanding the sound or sounds in question and how to change them will allow you to make the shift faster, so you can get back to the meaty part of scene work. As you work, remember that phonology is highly personal—it's the story of you and your people. There are some teachers, directors, agents even, who believe that you need to change your day-to-day accent in order to be a successful actor. In my professional opinion, that's an outdated way of thinking. If you want to change parts of your accent for whatever reason, that's great, and this book will help! But as long as you have ownership of your speech and can successfully perform in other accents with an appropriate amount of prep work, people in power shouldn't get to tell you that the accent you have offscreen is somehow going to keep you from working. Your best selling point as an artist is you, so why change something that is so profoundly yours?

RIVER OF SOUNDS

In this chapter, you're going to take your awareness of your speech anatomy to the next level. You'll learn about the possibilities for English speech sounds. You'll explore and notate the way you produce each sound. You'll practice exercises that will help you perform speech sounds with purpose, flexibility, and ease. Most important, you will not be told how your accent should sound.

Jumping in the river

Imagine for a moment that the air inside you is a body of water. Your lungs are great lakes. The trachea is a river that flows past the larynx and meets the delta of the mouth and nose. When you inhale, you draw air from the sea around you to your great lakes, and when you exhale the great lakes empty into the sea. Your vocal folds are like a dam along the path of that river—letting as much air pass as needed for whatever activity you're participating in. When you phonate, or make voice, the air is passing through that dam and moving it to create sound the way a waterfall passes over a turbine to create electricity. Your soft palate is like a switch—changing the direction of the flow along the delta to reach the sea via the nose or mouth or both. Speech at its most basic is changing the flow of this river to create individual sounds—phonemes—and string them together into syllables, words, and thoughts. Let's take a tour of phonology, or some of the ways we might play in this river.

Play: The shape of the river

1. With a relaxed vocal tract, take a breath and let it out slowly.
2. Repeat step 1, but this time, move your articulators around without bothering the flow of air too much.
3. Repeat step 2, adding voice to your exploration.
4. Now, with a relaxed vocal tract, release all your breath and then *inhale* slowly.
5. Repeat step 4, but this time, move your vocal tract around without bothering the flow of air too much.
6. Add voice while you *inhale*!

Flow is the first step to creating speech. All spoken languages use air moving out of or into the lungs at some point. In the previous exploration, you explored **egressive** flow, in which the air and vibration move from the lungs outward, and **ingressive** flow, in which the air and vibration move from the outside toward the lungs. Some languages in the world use ingressive flow to create actual, everyday speech sounds. English speech mostly utilizes egressive flow, saving ingressive for exclamations like those that may mean, "yes," "yikes," or "golly gee, I seem to have stubbed my little toe." Besides the direction of the flow, in this exercise you also explored the difference between **voiced phonemes** and **voiceless phonemes**. In English, we use both.

Play: River geography

1. Flow continuously while switching back and forth between voiced and voiceless flow.
2. Take thirty seconds to move the articulators to shape the flow without disrupting it. You might move your tongue, lips, velum, larynx, pharynx, etc., but be sure that the flow is continuous.
3. Take thirty seconds to disrupt the flow. Create obstacles in your river. Imagine white-water rapids, whirlpools, turbines, boulders, etc.
4. Stop the flow. Can you disrupt the river while it's not moving? Try throwing some rocks in it or splashing around.
5. Take thirty seconds to toggle between shapes and obstacles, voiced or voiceless, and flow or no flow. Mix and match.

Congratulations, you're speaking! In this exercise, you've discovered **vowels** and **consonants**. A vowel is pure flow—the shape of the air and vibration as they move through the vocal tract. Vowels are created by the phonation of the vocal folds traveling though the arcs and cups in the tongue and the rounding or relaxation of the lips. A consonant is created by using the articulators to disrupt voiced or voiceless flow in a variety of ways. You moved your articulators in gestures like the ones you've been isolating and formed different sounds. In this exercise you even explored two different styles of consonants, the **pulmonic consonants**, which obstruct the flow of

RIVER OF SOUNDS

breath coming from the lungs, and the **non-pulmonic consonants**, which are created without air from the lungs. The English soundscape officially includes vowels (which are always voiced when we're not whispering) and voiced and voiceless pulmonic consonants, but, *tsk, tsk, tsk,* sometimes we use non-pulmonic sounds while we're speaking anyway.

Take a peek at Figure 5, the chart of the International Phonetic Alphabet on page 111. The IPA is a tool to notate the sounds of human speech. Each symbol represents a phoneme, or an individual speech sound. I like to think of phonemes as individual speech actions. The goal of this book is not to teach you how to use IPA in all its specificity, but I find it useful to use the smaller charts within the IPA chart in order to conceptualize how we perform the sounds, which is our real focus. We'll work through the charts and play with the English sounds in each section. Let's start with vowels.

Vowel chart

Have a look at the chart labeled "Vowels." If you ignore all the symbols for a moment, you have a quadrilateral with points along the edges that divide each line evenly. Believe it or not, this is a two-dimensional map of the inside of your mouth, as if you were looking to the left. So, the labels "Front," "Central," and "Back" refer to the front, center, and back of the open space above your tongue and below the roof of your mouth. The labels "Close," "Close-mid," "Open-mid," and "Open" refer to the proximity of the tongue to the roof of the mouth. We care about this space because a vowel is created by curving the tongue toward or away from the roof of the mouth. Depending on the location of that curve in the front, center, or back of the mouth and the height or depth of that curve, we'll hear a different vowel. Last, we'll also hear a different vowel when the lips are rounded versus when they remain unrounded. Let's take the symbols into consideration for a moment. You'll notice that there are two symbols for every point on the chart. Symbols on the left of the point have unrounded lips, and symbols on the right have rounded lips. To recap, each vowel has three ingredients: the location of the curve in the front, center, or back of the tongue; the height of the curve; and the rounding or relaxation of the lips.

Exercise: Moving mountains

In this block of exercises, we're going to take the tongue-arching and cupping exercises and apply them to vowels. We're going to find the edges of the vowel space, which is the outermost line of the vowel chart. By rolling the arc or cup of the tongue through the extremes of the vowel space, you'll also strengthen the muscles of the tongue so it will become easier to shape vowels that you're not used to. This takes a long time to master, so feel free to practice for a little while using the companion videos in Appendix D, and then come back to it later.

1 Warming up the arches:

    a Scratch the length of your tongue along your upper front teeth to bring your awareness to the body of the tongue.

    b Scratch the length of your tongue on the alveolar ridge. Notice the shape of the body of the tongue.

    c Leave the tip of your tongue behind your bottom front teeth and touch the front of the body of your tongue to the back of the alveolar ridge (ten times).

    d Leave the tip of your tongue behind your bottom front teeth and touch the middle of the body of your tongue to the hard palate (ten times).

    e Leave the tip of your tongue behind your bottom front teeth and touch the back of the body of your tongue to the velum (ten times).

    f Leave the tip of your tongue behind your bottom front teeth and touch the front of the body of your tongue to the back of the alveolar ridge, then roll that point of contact back along the length of the palate all the way to the velum. I find it helps to imagine that single point of contact like a laser pointer moving along the roof of your mouth. If the contact feels larger than the laser pointer, relax the rest of your tongue down as a small point on your tongue makes contact.

    g Reverse the direction and roll the point of contact forward along the palate to the back of the alveolar ridge.

2. Finding the top of the vowel space:
   a. Whisper "EE." Feel the shape of your tongue as it arches behind the alveolar ridge. Inhale an "EE" to feel the cool air trace the shape of the arch.
   b. Touch the back of your tongue to your velum.
   c. Separate the back of your tongue from the velum just enough to inhale through. Feel the cool air trace the shape of the arch of the back of your tongue.
   d. Roll the arch of your tongue forward from the velum, along the palate, to the alveolar ridge, leaving just enough space to inhale through. You should end in that "EE" shape.
   e. Reverse the direction and roll your tongue back from "EE" to an arch just off of the velum. Can you hear the pitch of the air changing as you roll forward and back?
3. Making close vowels:
   a. Purse your lips tightly.
   b. Roll your tongue from the velum to the alveolar ridge while sending air through that space.
   c. Roll your tongue from the back of the alveolar ridge to the velum while sending air through that space. Notice the pitch of the air changing as you move from back to front and back again.
   d. Repeat while sending voice. Notice the changing vowel sounds you're creating.
   e. Relax your lips and repeat. Notice the new vowel sounds you're creating.
   f. When you really nail this exercise, you'll be rolling your tongue through all the close vowels on the vowel chart. You might even recognize some as sounds of your own accent. Look at a vowel chart and trace your finger along the top line to try to keep track of where you are inside your mouth.
4. Finding the back of the vowel space:
   a. Arch your tongue in the back toward the velum. Breathe in through that shape to feel the shape of the arch.

- **b** Say "AH" like you're at the doctor's office. Breathe in through that shape to feel the open space of the cup in the back of your tongue.
- **c** Move your tongue from that "AH" shape up toward the velum. You'll be moving from a cup to an arch. It's the same movement as if you were going to pronounce a "K" in slow motion but stopping before your tongue makes contact.
- **d** Reverse that and turn your arch near the velum to a cup in the back of the tongue.

5 Making back vowels:
- **a** Move your tongue from the "AH" shape to the velum and back.
- **b** Repeat while sending voice. Notice how you're sliding through vowels.
- **c** Round your lips and repeat. Allow your lips to open as you move toward the "AH" shape and to close as you move toward the velum. Notice the new vowels you're creating.

6 Finding the front of the vowel space:
- **a** Arch your tongue into the "EE" shape. Breathe in through that shape to feel the shape of the arch.
- **b** Open your mouth and make a cup in the front of your tongue like you could hold a drop of water there. Breathe in through that shape to feel the open space of the cup in the front.
- **c** Move your tongue from that cup shape up toward the "EE" shape. You'll be moving from a cup to an arch.
- **d** Reverse that and slide from the "EE" shape to the cup in the front of your tongue.

7 Making front vowels:
- **a** Move your tongue from the "EE" shape to the cup in the front of your tongue and back.
- **b** Repeat while sending voice. Notice how you're sliding through vowels.

- c Purse your lips and repeat. Allow your lips to open as you move toward the cup shape and to close as you move toward the "EE" shape. It won't sound like an "EE," but more like the French "UE" sound. Notice all the new vowels you're creating.
8 Making open vowels:
- a Roll your tongue from the "AH" cup in the back of your tongue to the cup in the front of your tongue.
- b Add voice. This movement will sound like you're sliding from one "AH" to another. I like to think of the front cup as sounding like the American Southern "EYE" sound, like in "*My my my*, sweet cherry *pie*."

You've now found the four corners of the vowel space and all the vowels in between them with both rounded and unrounded lips. If you pause anywhere during this exploration, you'll be speaking a vowel. Each horizontal line on the vowel chart represents a roughly even amount of space from open to closed, and each vertical line is a roughly even amount of space from front to back. The vowels heard at the intersections are called **cardinal vowels**, because they divide the vowel space evenly. I use the cardinal vowels as physical guideposts for finding other vowels. When I'm working with a new accent, I'll move from a cardinal vowel to the new vowel to really pinpoint my awareness of where the arch or cup is in my mouth. I can then visualize that placement using the vowel chart as a guide.

There's one more vowel that's extremely important that we haven't found yet. It's so important that it has a name: the **schwa**. The schwa is the vowel sound created by the lack of a cup or arch in the tongue. It is the direct center of the vowel chart.

Exercise: Finding schwa

1 Blow raspberries with your tongue to relax it.
2 Shake out your tongue.
3 Relax the tip of your tongue behind your lower front teeth.

4 Send voice through with a completely relaxed tongue. I write this sound as "uh," but I feel it like "eugh." It's the first sound of my pronunciation of "about" and the last sound of my pronunciation of "sofa." Do you use this sound in your accent?

Diphthongs

Some of what we think of as vowel sounds are actually a quick movement from one vowel to another. A phoneme that's created by moving from one vowel to another in the same syllable is called a **diphthong**. In the following exercise, you'll move from vowel to vowel to invent or possibly rediscover a few diphthongs.

Play: Inventing diphthongs

1 Touch one of the vowels in the column on the left as you pronounce it, then touch a random vowel from the column on the right as you pronounce it.

2 Now trace your finger from the vowel on the left to the vowel on the right as you slide from one vowel to the other.

3 Try going a little faster, so it sounds like the speed of a regular syllable. As you invent diphthongs in this way, you might recognize a combination or two.

AH	OO
EE	IH
EH	AW
AW	AH
OO	EE
IH	ER

4 Some dialects of English even have **triphthongs**, where you slide through three vowels in the same syllable. Repeat the above exercise and slide your finger through three of the vowels.

Lexical sets

If you were to ask how many vowels English has, most people would answer, "Six: A, E, I, O, U, and sometimes Y." But beyond the letters, English has a multitude of spoken vowel sounds. Add together the different vowels pronounced by different dialects of English and the vowels of English multiply. So, we need a system to talk about vowel sounds that takes all those variations into consideration. As a subset of phonology, the study of speech sounds in general is called **phonemics**. This is what we did when we counted the phonemes in the word "tack." We talked about a "T" sound, a vowel sound, and a "k" sound. Once we start talking about specific speech sounds, like the actual sounds that you make when you pronounce "tack" versus the actual sounds that I make when I pronounce "tack," we're suddenly talking about **phonetics**. We can describe the "T" sound that I make versus the "T" sound that you make.

When we're talking about vowels in general, vowel phonemics, we're going to use a system that linguist J. C. Wells came up with called **lexical sets**. A lexical set is a list of words that share the same vowel in any one accent. For example: I say the words "fleece," "bees," and "cheat" with the same vowel. Those three words would sound similar to one another when a person from Yorkshire pronounced all of them as well. Even though the vowel that I use for this list of words and the vowel that my friend from Yorkshire would use will be different from each other, we can describe the vowel in this group of words as a phoneme that's different, say, from the vowel in words like "dress," "head," and "left," so these words form a distinct lexical set. Instead of naming these groups of words as a sound like "EE," we just name them a word in that set, so we would say "fleece," "bees," and "cheat" belong to the FLEECE set, and "dress," "head," and "left" belong to the DRESS set.

Lexical sets are extremely useful when comparing accents, so we'll start here as we explore your individual accent. We'll begin by creating your **phonemic inventory**, or the list of lexical sets that you use. For instance, in my accent I would use the same vowel for words in the TRAP set as I would for words in the BATH set. So in my mind TRAP and BATH merge into the same phoneme. On the other hand, in my accent I would pronounce MAN and THANKS with two different vowels, so my phonemic inventory would include a TRAP/BATH merge, a MAN set, and a THANKS set. Some accents in the United Kingdom might have a TRAP/MAN/THANKS merge and a BATH set, and some accents from the Caribbean might have just one TRAP/BATH/MAN/THANKS merge. The three accents I've just described have three different phonemic inventories.

Idiolectsploration: Phonemic inventory of vowels

In the following exercise, you're going to compare words in your own accent in order to build the phonemic inventory of your idiolect. You'll come away from this exercise with an idea of what vowel categories you use and what kinds of words fall into each category. Later in this chapter, you'll explore the vowels in each lexical set and describe how you create them in your idiolect. By knowing your phonemic inventory, you can explore vowels set by set instead of word by word. Knowing your phonemic inventory will also make future accent work easier. Knowing that I merge the TRAP and BATH lists, in order to work on a London accent, I will have to separate those two lists in my mind. This exercise can be tedious because there are a lot of lexical sets to compare, but it's incredibly rewarding, because you'll come away with a deep understanding of how you use vowel sounds in your accent.

1. Using Table 5, speak each lexical set word and then compare it to all the other lexical set words. If there is another lexical set word that you pronounce the same way, write that word in the merge box. For instance, I would say, "Trap, fleece. Trap, kit. Trap, dress. Trap, bath." Since I pronounce "bath" with the same vowel I use to pronounce "trap," I would write "bath" in the merge box next to "TRAP." *Note: in lexical sets with an asterisk next to them, we're exploring the unstressed syllable and not the stressed syllable.

TABLE 5 *Phonemic Inventory of Vowels*

Lexical set	Merge
FLEECE	
KIT	
DRESS	

RIVER OF SOUNDS

TRAP
BATH
commA*
lettER*
STRUT
NURSE
GOOSE
TUNE
FOOT
Obey*
THOUGHT
CLOTH
LOT
FAther
FACE
PRICE
CHOICE
GOAT
MOUTH
NEAR
SQUARE
CURE
NORTH
FORCE
adMIRE
POWER

Note: *Indicates a lexical set in which we're exploring the unstressed syllable.

2   The following group of words are lexical sets that I've added over the years as I've worked on dialects with different phonemic inventories. Compare these words to the lexical sets in Table 5 and add them to the main sets when they share the vowel. If any of these lexical sets are pronounced differently than all the other lexical sets, then that extra set is part of your phonemic inventory and you can add it to Table 5.

FEEL, hapPY*, SINGING, BEtween*, raTED*, PEN, HEAD, busiNESS*, THANKS, LOVE, CURL, CURRY, Olympic*, POOL, FULL, ULTRA, THAW, PALM, FAIL, PRIZE, AISLE, GOAL, COIL, MERRY, MARRY, MARY

3   Listen to your recording of the word list from Chapter 1. Are there any words there that you would say have their own lexical set? You can add those now!

Vowel phonetics

Now that you have the phonemic inventory of the vowels you use, you can go through and map all these sounds by noting how you actually pronounce them. This is particularly useful if you ever need to change one or more of the sounds you speak for a role. Making a phonetic map of your vowels also builds awareness of your own vocal tract. This awareness, in turn, will benefit your voicework, singing, and even movement since the tongue and muscles of the throat are so connected to the spine. There's an immense amount of exploration you can do with these vowels, so I recommend doing a little bit at a time. Play with one lexical set for a little while and figure out how your body creates that sound, and then the next time you're curious, you can do another lexical set. I would skip the lexical sets that have "R" involved, like NURSE and START. "Rs" can be quite the can of worms, so they'll have their own section in Chapter 9.

Vowel mapping is also a fun way to explore the IPA vowel chart, so if a deeper understanding of IPA as a tool to describe sounds is a goal of yours, now's the time to hone those skills by describing your sounds with IPA symbols. Last, this exploration is exactly how I approach the vowels of new accents as well. First I create a phonemic inventory for the new accent, and then I map the phonetics using the following steps. So, if dialect and accent work is something that interests you, once you hone your awareness of your own accent, you can use these same steps to learn about new accents as well.

Idiolectsploration: Vowel mapping

1. Speak the name of the lexical set you'd like to work on. No need to go in any particular order. Follow your curiosity. For example, I might start with TRAP.

2. Say this lexical set word in slow motion. Notice the movement of your articulators.

3. Count the phonemes of this word. For TRAP, I have four phonemes: a "T," an "R," the vowel of interest, and a "P."

4. Speak just the vowel of interest. Notice what your tongue and lips are doing.

5. Do your tongue and/or lips move over the course of the vowel? If your lips and tongue hold their shape for the duration of this vowel, it is a monophthong. If your lips or tongue move over the course of the sound, you're pronouncing a diphthong or triphthong. If that's the case, you'll repeat steps 6–17 in order to identify each vowel that you move through. Note that some diphthongs are very subtle. My GOOSE set starts with unrounded lips and quickly moves to rounded lips.

6. Whisper the vowel (or whichever vowel in the sequence of movements you're working on if you're dealing with a diphthong or triphthong). Feel the warm air traveling over your tongue. I like to think of the air painting my tongue to help me see the shape of my tongue in my mind's eye.

7. Inhale the vowel. Feel the cool air traveling over your tongue and painting the shape of your tongue.

8. Is your tongue in an arching, mountain-like shape or in a cup shape? If you're exploring the IPA, the arching vowels will be found in the top half of the chart and the cupping vowels will be found in the lower half of the chart. Remember, this is a map

of the vowel space inside your mouth and the IPA notates the most extreme point of the curve of your tongue.

9 How high or low is your mountain or cup? Is it as high or low as it goes, or in the middle somewhere? Describe this height or depth as "close" for a high arch, "close-mid" for a small arch, "open-mid" for a small cup, or "open" for a large cup.

10 Revisit the moving mountains exercise (earlier in this chapter) to find the far reaches of the vowel space. Trace your finger across the vowel chart as you go to have a rough idea of where your arch or cup is in the vowel space.

11 Slide from each of the corners to your vowel while tracing your finger along that same path on the vowel chart. In which direction do you have to move the arch or cup from each corner to get to your vowel?

12 Find the schwa by shaking out your tongue and letting it relax completely.

13 Slide from the schwa to your vowel while tracing your finger along that same path on the vowel chart. In which direction does the mountain or cup have to move to get to your vowel?

14 Is your vowel in the front of the mouth (toward ultimate "EE"), in the back of the mouth (toward ultimate "OO"), or in the center of mouth, closer to the schwa? Describe this horizontal placement as "front," "central," or "back."

15 Speak your vowel and notice your lips. Are they rounded or unrounded? Note that.

16 If you're using the IPA, you now have a general area on the vowel chart where you feel this vowel and you know if it's rounded or unrounded. Find the closest symbol to your vowel, remembering that rounded sounds are on the right of the point and unrounded are on the left of the point. You can stop there, or if you want to be really descriptive, you can add /+/ under the symbol if your vowel is farther in front of the point in the chart; /–/ if your vowel is farther back than the point on the chart / ˌ/ if your vowel is higher than the symbol, and / ˌ/ if your vowel is lower than the symbol.

17 If you're working on a diphthong or triphthong, move in slow motion to the next vowel and trace your finger along that trajectory on the vowel chart. This will give you an idea of where to start the exploration of that second or third vowel.

18 Make a list of other words that have this vowel and speak them out loud. Feel how the shape of the vowel responds to new consonants both before and after the vowel.

Exercise: Vowel practice

If you're interested in exploring the basic lexical sets, you can use the following words, sentences, and short poems. Feel free to add any of these practice materials to your daily warm-up if there's a specific sound that you're targeting or if you want to add variety to the texts you use. I wrote almost all of these ones, so, again, they're in my voice. Feel free to write your own in your voice! I'd love to see what you come up with! Remember as you go through that your phonemic inventory might merge a few of these lexical sets or separate a few of these lexical sets into multiple sets. As you practice with these materials, notice any outliers. My TRAP set is all over the place!

FLEECE

1 even, eke, pea, peek, dean, deep, key, keep, beguine, geese, me, meet, feeble, feet, vegan, vitae, theme, thief, these, seed, seek, zebra, Ezekiel, sheen, chic, aubergine, cheese, chief, congeal, Jeep, heave, heat, league, leap, grieve, reek, ye, yeast, wheel, wheat, we, weep.

2 Even Rita retweets Stephen's grievances.

3 We were greedy for Beanie Babies in the nineteen nineties.

4 The green team was deemed supreme by the magazine in Leeds.

5 The mean streets of Gina's dreams,

Teem with beasts or so it seems.

She feeds them veal and leafy greens,

To keep them meaty, strong, and lean.

KIT

1. ill, issue, pink, pick, bib, bit, stiff, tincture, dim, dip, kiss, kilt, give, git, mill, mix, nibs, knit, fin, fish, Victor, vision, thick, thimble, this, sin, sister, zinfandel, zit, shin, ship, chill, chicken, jig, gist, hidden, history, lid, lip, shrill, wrist, yin, yippee, whim, whip, wig, wick.
2. Tim twiddled his fingers in anticipation of the film.
3. The itchy hippo is allergic to the thistle in the distance.
4. Elizabeth gifted Minerva with a picture of the Big Dipper.
5. Is this the isthmus I wished for at Christmas,

   Or is this a different gift off my wish list?

   If Izzy and Jimmy got piglets and chickens,

   Then I want my isthmus or else I will sicken.

DRESS

1. egg, etch, pen, pest, beg, bet, tell, tech, dentist, deck, Kent, kept, again, get, men, met, negative, next, fend, festival, vent, vest, Thelma, theft, them, sell, session, zed, zest, shell, chef, cherry, check, gel, eject, head, hex, leg, lest, rebel, rest, yen, yes, when, whet, well, west.
2. Debbie left the rec center and went to the festival instead.
3. For a healthy life, it's recommended to tend to general wellness by one's twenties.
4. Eddie lamented when he dented Brenda's Chevrolet.
5. The battle was finished and then,

   Toys were hid in the attic again.

   Generations whip past.

   Lead hearts sing aghast,

   "The Fugue of the Sad Tin Men."

TRAP

1. azure, ax, pad, pack, badge, back, tan, tack, dad, daffy, gal, gap, magic, mash, nab, knack, fad, fact, valiant, vaccine, thatch, than, that, sad, sack, zag, zap, shadow, shack, Chad, chap, jab, Jack, haggle, hack, lamb, lash, rally, rack, yam, yak, whammy, whack, wag, quack.
2. That bad cat actually tackled the ambassador.
3. Al has a natural knack with palindromes and other patterns.
4. Tad was ravenous, so he had a stack of pancakes in the cafeteria.
5. The angry man laughed at the bank,

    That the *Titanic* had passed and tragically sank.

    He danced, clapped, and ran,

    'Til the bankers spat, "Banned!"

    Then he gasped in his tracks and he ran home and drank.
6. The daffy gadget made of wax,

    Lacks razzle-dazzle. 'Tis bafflingly lax.

    It cannot snap matches, vacuum, or fax,

    But racks up a bill of a thousand plus tax.

BATH

1. answer, ask, path, past, bath, bask, staff, task, daft, dance, can't, cast, gasp, ghastly, command, mask, nasty, fast, advance, vast, sample, disaster, example, shaft, shan't, chant, chance, half, enhance, glance, glass, trance, craft, raspberry.
2. The giraffe in the photograph pranced in the grass.
3. The castle held fast as the avalanche advanced.
4. I demand a cask of the raspberry drink I sampled in your flask.
5. The afternoon passed as we basked in the grass;

    The pasture enchanted while dusk settled fast.

The branches of trees gently danced in the breeze;
The day slipped our grasp as the night fell at last.

COMMA*

(Reminder: we are interested in the unstressed syllable, the schwa)

1. about, oppose, pedantic, campus, banana, tuba, tonight, staccato, lambda, tandem, condition, capacious, saga, spigot, drama, Christmas, Barnum, nefarious, ferocious, sofa, larva, veneer, euthanasia, Ithaca, balsa, support, visa, resurrect, Russia, fuchsia, amnesia, luxury, spatula, postulate, Georgia, geranium, Havana, inhalation, atlas, proclamation, zebra, opera, ocular, billion, quota.
2. The capable panda ate eucalyptus in Tulsa.
3. "Gallop apace!" Stella asserts from the sofa.
4. The zealot volunteered for flagellation in the plaza.
5. Negronis and vodka were flowing all right,
   But they blamed the tequila for the campus-wide fight.
   The moderation of saints is the only constraint,
   To safely consume margaritas at night.

LETTER*

(Reminder: we are interested in the unstressed syllable)

1. permit, percent, tuber, Shubert, countermand, sister, hinder, underpants, baker, curtail, linger, dagger, stammer, mercurial, energy, corner, singer, hanger, ferment, effort, lover, verbose, author, ether, mother, rather, blazer, zirconia, dasher, kosher, azure, Chernobyl, nature, germane, manager, hermetic, herculean, collar, lawyer, terror, horror, buyer, seer.
2. Shubert's concert was rather soporific.
3. My brother is the manager of barbershops in Berlin and Hamburg.
4. The effervescent Virginia was verbose while I stammered in the corner.

5 My brother, the tinker, had badgered my sister,
For finding her fingerprints on his transistor.
His zingers pervaded, her dressers were raided,
Until she perfected her role as resistor.

NURSE

1 err, irk, pearl, perch, bird, birth, turn, terse, derby, dirty, curl, Kirk, girl, gherkin, merge, mirth, nerd, nurture, fern, first, verb, vertigo, third, thirst, absurd, search, Lucerne, exertion, sherbet, shirk, churn, church, gerbil, jerk, learn, lurch, yearn, yurt, word, worst.

2 Bert returned from church thirty minutes before curfew.

3 Shirley hurt her neck rehearsing the Turkey Lurkey with fervor.

4 Birds perch in birch trees in the Berkshires.

5 The German girl twirled with verve,
But pearl-clutching jerks said she had some nerve.
She spun one last turn, then she hurled them a burn,
"Curb your curt cursing! Oh, when will you learn?"

STRUT

1 under, up, pun, puck, bug, bust, stung, touch, dug, dull, cousin, cup, gun, guppy, mud, much, snub, enough, fun, fuss, convulse, thumb, thus, sundry, such, Zuckerberg, shove, shutter, chum, chuck, jug, just, hull, hush, love, luck, runt, rough, yum, yuck, what, wonder.

2 Pumpkin and honeydew are cousins.

3 One must suffer yucky supper sometimes.

4 My husband was touchy after my rushing culminated in nothing.

5 A pudgy pug puppy tussled with a duck,
And got his tummy muddy from running in the muck.
His mummy gave a shrug as he rubbed it on the rug,
And hustled with the suds, as she sulked, "Well just my luck!"

GOOSE

1. ooze, oops, spoon, pooch, booze, boot, two, toot, doom, doofus, cool, scooter, gouda, goop, move, moose, noon, snooty, food, fool, soothe, sushi, zoom, gadzooks, shoe, shoot, choose, June, juice, who, hoop, lose, loot, rule, spruce, huge, youth, woo, whoop.
2. It's true; I threw two blue shoes at you.
3. The goose soufflé is Chef June's oeuvre.
4. I shooed the loon out of the rooster's coop with a pool noodle.
5. For whom do you pine and brood?
   Your pooch thinks your absence too rude.
   It's taken to chewing. Soon it'll be pooing.
   I'm afraid the dog's choosing to feud.

TUNE

1. stew, tulip, attitude, dubious, deduce, residue, news, nuclear, minutiae, elude, salute, revolution, enthusiastic.
2. The duke was an enthusiastic student.
3. The Tuesday newspaper had an astute review of *The Magic Flute*.
4. The tutor worked under a pseudonym to elude his union dues.
5. A tutor who tooted a flute,
   Tried to tutor two tooters to toot.
   Said the two to the tutor, "Is it harder to toot,
   Or to tutor two tooters to toot?"[2]

FOOT

1. pudding, put, bull, book, bushes, stood, took, could, cushion, good, mushy, full, foot, forsook, soot, should, sugar, shook, hood, hook, plural, look, rural, rook, woman, woof.

---

[2]Wells, *The Jingle Book*.

2 Put the mushy pudding in the bushes.
3 The woman cushioned my broken foot on the book.
4 Should a good Wookie have hooves?
5 Pull out a book and have a look.
   Could you find me a new kind of dish I could cook?
   I'm tired of cooking just kugel and pudding
   And wasting the skills from the class that I took.

THOUGHT

1 awe, awkward, paw, pauper, ball, bought, tall, talk, dawn, daughter, cause, calk, gaunt, gawk, mall, maw, gnaw, naughty, fawn, fought, avaunt, thaw, thought, saw, sauce, exhausted, shawl, chaw, chalk, jaw, hall, hawk, lawn, applaud, raw, wrought, yawn, wall, walk.
2 Audrey bought baubles at the mall.
3 I thought our walk would exhaust my daughter, but I'm the one yawning.
4 Call to talk about the wrought-iron awning.
5 Shawn was too bawdy and awkwardly called,
   To Aubrey who paused, exhausted—appalled!
   We gawked when we saw Shawn get punched in the jaw.
   And off Aubrey walked. While Shawn, he was sprawled.

CLOTH

1 offer, Australia, porridge, borrow, boss, tongs, historical, dog, coroner, cough, gong, categorical, moral, moth, metaphorical, foster, thong, authority, song, soft, chocolate, majority, horrify, lorry, lost, wrong, across, quarrel, warrant.
2 Florida oranges are often sold in Boston.
3 The warrior had a strong moral compass.
4 Tomorrow, we'll have Austrian chocolate porridge.

5   The wind had tossed the lorry aloft.
    We could only wish that the landing was soft.
    It landed on moss. We prepared for a loss.
    But our sorrow was early, the driver had off.

LOT

1   opt, on, pod, pox, boggy, box, stodgy, stock, don, dock, cod, gosh, modern, mop, novice, knock, fodder, fop, vomit, volley, solder, sopping, shock, shot, chop, job, jostle, holly, hock, lodge, slop, rock, robber, yonder, whopper, wobble, wash.
2   Ron opted to stop eating and box his bok choy.
3   The novice got the most modern goggles but forgot to practice.
4   Mom mocked the Klingons and Romulans nonstop.
5   Stop your sobbing, Tommy Todd,
    Your taste in Popsicles is odd.
    I do not mock, but I cannot stock,
    A lollipop that tastes of cod.

FATHER

1   almond, spa, pasta, balm, Bach, ta, taco, Dalí, calm, staccato, Ghana, legato, imam, mafia, father, bravado, façade, Sasha, zafu, shaman, horchata, java, maharani, salami, lava, drama, yacht, guava, waffle, wasp.
2   I got a calm massage at a spa in Prague.
3   As I wandered through Guatemala, I got hooked on guava.
4   You can get pasta, tacos, challah, or saag on La Cienega.
5   The naughty father robbed the spot,
    Where Sumatran Java is bought by the pot.
    The sauce fiend was calmly stopped by a cop,
    Who yawned, "Hurrah," then asked for a drop.

FACE

1. aid, ace, spade, paste, bay, bake, stain, steak, day, date, cable, cake, gain, gate, amaze, mace, knave, naked, fame, fake, veil, vape, thane, theta, they, say, sake, Zane, shave, shake, chain, chaste, jail, Jake, haze, haste, lame, lake, reign, rate, yay, whey, whale, way, waste.
2. I wasted a day's pay on a fake briefcase.
3. Hey, stay away from the great Salt Lake.
4. Make payments while your radio stays in layaway.
5. I remain afraid of that fateful day,
   I gazed on a haint at Camp Sleep-a-Way
   Blue paint and sage, and a newspaper page,
   Are the three main ways to hold spirits at bay.

PRICE/PRIZE

1. I'm, ice, pile, pike, bind, bite, tile, type, dive, diaper, kind, kite, guide, poltergeist, my, mice, nine, nice, file, fight, visor, invite, thigh, thy, side, sight, xylophone, zeitgeist, shy, shite, chide, jive, hide, hype, line, like, ride, rifle, yipes, why, white, wine, quite.
2. I'd like to tie-dye my advisor's bowtie.
3. The shy guy rides a motorbike.
4. Why don't I have nine lives like a feline?
5. Two white mice are locked in fight
   For who the ripe old cheese will bite.
   It's only rind, they soon will find,
   But they might finish out of spite.

GOAT

1. open, old, pole, poke, bone, boast, toe, stoke, dome, dote, code, coast, goes, gopher, mole, most, no, note, foam, folk, vogue, vocal, cathode, those, zone, show, chauffeur, chose,

choke, Joe, joke, home, host, low, elope, road, croak, yodel, yolk, won't, woeful.

2. Mona broke her oboe in the snow.
3. Joe spoke about Rome at the old folks' home.
4. I hope the road to Dover is open in November.
5. A toast to the gopher digging holes.

    It's woefully close to its end-of-year goals.

    A trophy, I hope, will appease that old dope,

    So alone it will leave my manicured knolls.

CHOICE

1. ointment, oyster, point, poise, boy, boisterous, toil, hoity-toity, doyenne, doily, coy, coin, goiter, moist, annoy, noise, foible, foist, void, voice, *Soylent Green*, soil, bok choy, choice, enjoy, joist, ahoy, hoist, purloin, ploy, thyroid, royal, opioid.
2. Troy hoisted the doyenne out of the soil.
3. Avoid pointing out how oily Joyce's soy and bok choy is.
4. Roy is poised to make some coin with his voice.
5. In Detroit there sang five boys,

    Whose melody never annoys.

    The fans were so loyal; thought the Jacksons were royal.

    Radios bring such joys.

MOUTH

1. owl, oust, power, spouse, bound, about, town, stout, dowry, douse, cowl, couch, gown, gout, mound, mouse, noun, snout, foul, Faust, vow, devout, thou, without, sow, shout, chowder, chow, jowl, joust, hound, house, plow, lout, round, grout, yowl, wow.
2. How can you proudly vow to be without chowder?
3. I'm astounded that the foul-mouthed scoundrel has a spouse.

4   The plow is housed outside the town.

5   There once lived a count with a hound,
He'd allowed to get much too round.
"Get out, you lout!" he growled with a pout,
"I'm taking you down to the pound!"

NEAR

1   Ear, earful, peer, pierce, beard, beer, steer, tear, deer, endear, kir, Kirsten, gear, smear, mere, sneer, fear, fierce, veer, sear, brassier, sheer, cheerleader, jeer, hear, hearsay, clear, leer, rear, arrears, year, weird, we're.

2   Bashir's endearing tears pierced Kirsten's heart.

3   It appears the steers are fierce beer drinkers.

4   My dear, I fear the mirepoix has been seared.

5   I reared a sweet yearling dear,
Who appeared to have no fear.
It ran to a clearing well past my hearing,
And was narrowly missed by a spear.

SQUARE

1   air, heir, pear, despair, bear, barefoot, stair, tears, dare, care, scarce, mare, snare, fair, Verdi, there, Azeri, share, chair, concerto, hair, hairspray, blare, clairvoyant, rarebit, prayer, where, aware, swear.

2   Claire scarcely cared about their hair.

3   I swear, I've had my fair share of rarebit.

4   Be careful not to scare the rare hare.

5   The daredevil carefully shared,
By zir latest feat ze was scared.
Ze'd accepted a dare. "Play a concerto; first chair!"
But now ze felt glaringly bared.

CURE

1. Urdu, poor, boorish, bourgeois, tour, dour, Coors, gourd, gourmet, moors, Darfur, sure, assure, mature, lure, allure, you're, secure.
2. Surely the tournament is insured.
3. I procured an obscure gourd.
4. You're secure in your allure.
5. There lives an old boor on the moor,
   Who loves his drink to be pure.
   He loudly abjures bourgeois drinks like Light Coors,
   But it's all that he can procure.

NORTH

1. organ, orchid, important, porpoise, born, border, storm, torque, adorn, scorn, corpse, gorge, Mormon, mortar, normal, snort, form, fork, cavort, thorn, assorted, consort, absorb, resort, shorn, short, George, horn, horse, lord, York, wardrobe, warp.
2. It's important to not resort to short retorts.
3. The warlock morphed Morgan into a thorn.
4. The mortar scorched the fortified fortress.
5. George was remorseful he'd shorn,
   The corporal's torso one morn.
   His short wiry form just couldn't stay warm,
   Bare as the day he was born.

FORCE

1. ore, pore, sport, boar, board, tore, notorious, door, adore, score, court, gore, Gregorian, more, mourn, ignore, snort, afford, forth, divorce, thorax, sore, sword, absorbent, shore, shorn, chore, chortle, hoar, hoarse, explore, deplore, roar, yore, wore, sworn.

RIVER OF SOUNDS

2   The floorboards were notoriously porous.
3   The Gregorian court explored choral chanting.
4   I implore you to explore the glorious memorial.
5   The flora must not be ignored.
    It must be shorn with a sword.
    I'll yell till I'm hoarse, but won't do it of course.
    And for that, I'm all but deplored.

START

1   arm, art, par, spark, bard, barf, tar, starch, darn, dark, card, cart, garb, Garth, marble, march, snarl, snarky, farm, farce, varnish, varsity, sardines, sergeant, tsar, shard, sharp, char, chart, jar, jargon, harm, heart, alarm, lark, yard, yarn.
2   It's hard to carve a scarf out of marble.
3   Don't start with your jargon, Marvin.
4   It was alarming to see Marsha varnish the large sardine jar.
5   A shar-pei named Charlie would bark,
    And guard his parcel of park.
    Other dogs he'd alarm, but he meant them no harm.
    He was ardently making his mark.

ADMIRE

1   ire, expire, umpire, buyer, attire, tired, dire, gyre, mire, fire, pacifier, sire, desire, shire, hire, flier, supplier, friar, prior, choir, require.
2   The tired umpire was required to retire.
3   The air purifier's wire caught fire.
4   I need dryer attire that won't make me perspire.
5   Sire, the spire's on fire.
    But the crier is stuck in a mire.
    Should I call for the choir, and inspire their ire?
    Please tell me, what do you require?

POWER

1. hour, our, empower, bower, tower, dower, scour, coward, Gower, devour, sour, shower, Howard, flour, flower, glower.
2. Howard devoured the cauliflower.
3. The coward cowered in the tower.
4. Eisenhower's flowers could use a shower.
5. There once was a glowering flower,

   Who wanted to snatch garden power.

   It proved a great coward, and then got devoured,

   And left naught behind as a dower.

9
SPLASHING IN THE RIVER

The vowels that you use hold so much potential for expression. When you use a pitch change to get what you need, it's the vowel that really sings. When you add length to the stressed syllable of an image, it's the vowel that stretches. But if you spoke in vowels alone, you would be difficult to understand. Consonants help you add specificity to your meaning, so your thoughts are understood. They help you create the rhythms you use to add context to your thought. They also hold clues about your identity.

Now that you have an understanding of some or all of the vowels that you use, we'll go through a similar process for the consonant sounds. Take a peek back at the IPA chart (Figure 5 on page 111). We'll now zero in on the pulmonic consonant chart and the consonants that you create with air from your lungs. There are three ingredients to a pulmonic consonant (this will be on the proverbial test): *placement*, *manner*, and *voicing*. Each column tells us the **placement of articulation**, or the articulators involved in making each sound in that column.

- **Bilabial**—using two lips
- **Labiodental**—using the bottom lip and the top teeth
- **Dental**—using the tip or blade of the tongue and the teeth
- **Alveolar**—using the tip or blade of the tongue and the alveolar ridge

- **Postalveolar**—using the tip or blade of the tongue between the alveolar ridge and the palate
- **Retroflex**—curling the tip or blade of the tongue back toward the palate
- **Palatal**—using the body of the tongue and the palate
- **Velar**—using the body of the tongue and the velum (soft palate)
- **Uvular**—using the back of the tongue and the uvula
- **Pharyngeal**—using the root of the tongue straight back toward the back wall of the pharynx (throat)
- **Glottal**—using the vocal folds

If you look at each box on the chart, you'll notice that some boxes contain two symbols. This is our hidden twist—voicing. Whenever you have two consonants sharing a box, they have the same placement and manner, but the sound on the right is performed while the vocal folds are in close proximity and vibrating, whereas the sound on the left is performed while the vocal folds are open and not vibrating. Because they share the same placement and manner, we call these sounds **cognate pairs**. As you've probably guessed by now, each row tells us the **manner of articulation**, or what type of gesture creates those sounds. Each row of consonants is performed in the same manner, but in the placement noted by each column. We'll go into detail about each manner in the following sections, but scan the chart for symbols you recognize as letters and see if you can begin to guess the meaning of each manner of articulation.

For the upcoming sections, we'll also need one symbol from the "other symbols" section of the chart, which houses sounds that are created with placement and manner combinations that don't fit neatly on the chart and need a symbol of their own. We'll also play with some specific sounds and qualities that we could note with **diacritics** and **suprasegmentals**. Diacritics are used to note specificities in the placement, manner, or voicing of the sound that makes it a little different from what can be assumed from the symbol found on the chart. Suprasegmentals don't note changes in the sound they attach to, just the quality or quantity of the sound. We've already used three: primary stress, secondary stress, and syllable break.

Plosives

Plosives, or stop-plosives, occur when the airflow from the lungs is completely blocked by articulators in the vocal tract and is then released, creating the characteristic popping noise. The popping noise will change depending on which articulators make contact and block the air.

Play: Freeform plosives

1. Inhale with an open mouth. Exhale on a gentle "H" sound and use different articulators to block the flow of that "H," and then release the articulators to get back to the "H." Make sure that you've created a real seal and no air is allowed to escape your nose.
2. Repeat with voice. Hold out an "UH" sound and use different articulators to block the flow, and then release back into "UH."
3. How many different articulator combinations can you find that block the air?

As you explored earlier, plosives can be voiced or voiceless. For a plosive to be voiced, the vocal folds vibrate a split second before the explosion. Voiceless plosives don't vibrate the vocal folds before the explosion, which makes them silent until the explosion happens. Try going back and forth between "P" and "B" to hear the difference. The English phonemic inventory includes three voiced and three voiceless plosives in cognate pairs. /p, b/, /t, d/, / k, g/.

After the explosion, a voiced plosive explodes into whatever vowel sound comes after it, or a very short, relaxed schwa /ə/ if it's the last sound before a pause. In voiceless plosives, you might hear the next vowel sound directly after the explosion, or you might hear a puff of air between the explosion and the start of the vowel. This puff of air is called **aspiration**. Different versions of the same phoneme, like an aspirated or unaspirated "T" sound, are called **allophones.** Different accents of English will have different rules about when to aspirate voiceless plosives and when not to, but most will aspirate the consonants more often than not and won't aspirate voiceless plosives if they're in a consonant cluster after "S."

Exercise: Recognizing plosives

Work with a partner or record yourself speaking the following word list. First identify if you're pronouncing a /t/ or a /d/ sound. If you're pronouncing a "D," mark the word with [d]. If you hear a "T" sound, you'll need to decide which allophone of /t/ you're really pronouncing. Speak the word again with your hand in front of your mouth, feeling for the "puff of H" aspiration on your hand. Mark the word with [tʰ] for an aspirated "T" and [t] for an unaspirated "T." If you hear something else that doesn't fit these categories, mark the word with a question mark.

tab____ stab____ dab____ attire____ adorn____ astern____
lat____ last____ lad____ better____ caddy____ batman____

Idiolectsploration: Plosive aspiration

Let's expand this exploration. In this exercise, record yourself speaking the following word list. Listen to the recording and mark which allophone you're saying for the underlined consonant. Feel free to describe what you're hearing with words, or you can use the key to describe what you're hearing with the IPA. If you notice anything that doesn't fit into one of the categories in the key, mark it with a question mark.

Key:

Voiceless, unaspirated plosives /p, t, k/
Voiceless, aspirated plosives /pʰ, tʰ, kʰ/
Voiced plosives /b, d, g/
Plosives with no audible release /p̚, t̚, k̚, b̚, d̚, g̚/

/t, d/: tick ___ steak ___ actor ___ ate ___
aid ___ try ___ mists ___ drank ___
/p, b/: boy ___ poi ___ spot ___ stopper ___ quip ___
nab ___ pray ___ play ___ braid ___
/k, g/: call ___ gab ___ gray ___ bagger ___ tack ___
crab ___ packer ___ clay ___ quest ___

> Let's look for some patterns.
>
> 1. Look at all the voiced plosives. Are there any that are spelled in a way that surprised you?
> 2. Look at the plosives clustered after "S." Are they usually aspirated, unaspirated, or voiced?

SPLASHING IN THE RIVER

3. Look at the voiceless sounds before stressed syllables. Are they aspirated or unaspirated?
4. Look at the voiceless sounds before unstressed syllables. Are they usually aspirated or unaspirated?
5. Look at the voiceless sounds that start a word. Are they usually aspirated or unaspirated?
6. Do you notice any patterns about plosives when they're the last sound of a word?
7. If you have any question marks, do you discern any patterns? What sounds are near the question marks?

No audible release

During that idiolectsploration, you may have felt like the plosive just stopped the flow and didn't explode at all. This is called **no audible release**. If you tried to explode every plosive in the sentence "D̲ad c̲an't create great po̲pcorn," you could run out of breath before the end and it would definitely sound overlabored. In order to speak in strings of uninterrupted sounds, we don't always explode plosives before other hard consonants. Try that sentence again, but explode only the plosives that have a vowel or "R" sound after them. Next, try exploding all the plosives in the sentence "I can't type pink characters." Tough, right? Say that sentence again in your own accent. I'm guessing that you only exploded one "T," one "P," and one "K" when two of these sounds were next to each other. The no-audible-release rule works here as well when you have two of the same plosives next to each other, but the result feels a little bit different.

Play: Linking plosives

When you have two of the same plosives or cognates next to each other, you can hold the explosion of the first one for a beat and then explode the second one. This is called **gemination** and it sounds like a single, slow-motion plosive. Try it with some of these phrases.

Pop pays   stop biting   drab buttons   can't type   bad time
dad drives   kick cans   pack gum   long game

Glottal plosives

There's another important plosive that we haven't talked about yet, the glottal plosive, or a plosive sound created by closing the vocal folds and then releasing them. You might hear a director, teacher, or music director refer to this sound as a glottal attack or a glottal stop. This sound is fairly ubiquitous in accents of English, but different accents use this sound in different ways. Let's find it!

Play: When glottals attack!

1. Open your mouth and take a deep breath.
2. Hold your breath without closing your mouth or moving your tongue.
3. Let the air go. Did you feel a popping sensation in your throat? That was a glottal plosive.
4. Send a stream of voice and interrupt it with glottal plosives: "uh-uh-uh-uh-uh-uh-uh."

Idiolectsploration: Glottal plosives

There are a few different ways that you might use a glottal plosive in your accent. The first use is common in the United Kingdom, and that's when a glottal plosive is used as the pronunciation of "T" when the "T" sound comes between two vowels. English speakers all across the globe may also use a glottal plosive with no audible release when a "T" is the last sound of a thought or phrase. Last, speakers may also use a glottal plosive in front of words that begin with a vowel sound when the thought or phrase begins with a vowel, to emphasize the word that begins with a vowel sound, or simply to link from one vowel to another. Read the following list of words while listening and feeling for the glottal plosive. Mark each word with [ʔ] for the glottal plosive, [tʰ] for an aspirated "T," [t] for an unaspirated "T," or ? for something else.

[ʔ], [tʰ], [t], or ?: kitten___ sitting___ water___ bottle___
        fitted___ pita___ patty___
[ʔ], [tʰ], [t], or ?: fit___ Scott___ late___ kite___
        what___ smart ___ feet___

SPLASHING IN THE RIVER

[?] or nothing: uh-oh___ always___ all alone___
    We AREN'T going?___ it is___

Exercise: Plosive practice

1. Release your jaw using the exercises under "Exercise: Release" in Chapter 5. The following exercises should be completed with a relaxed jaw.

2. Release your tongue by blowing air through your tongue and lips, first without voice and then with voice.

3. Isolate your lips by trumpeting them forward as far as they go, then release (ten times).

4. Isolate your lips by pursing them in toward each other, and then release (ten times).

5. Isolate your lips by combining the two. Hold your lips forward and then purse them together and release (ten times).

6. Isolate your lips with blotting. Hold the taut edge of a clean piece of paper to your lip corners. Blot your lips on the paper and release without gripping in your jaw. Try blotting harder and harder without gripping or closing your jaw.

7. Release your jaw open wide enough to fit one finger between your molars from the outside of your cheeks. Hold your fingers there.

8. Isolate your tongue by firmly pressing the tip or blade to the alveolar ridge without biting down on your fingers (ten times).

9. Activate the back of your tongue by saying "Kick. Kick. Kah." /kʰɪk‿kʰɪk‿kʰɑ/ Start slowly and then speed this up.

10. Activate the back of your tongue by saying "Gig. Gig. Gah." /gɪg‿gɪg‿gɑ/ Start slowly and then speed this up.

11. Activate

    a Dactyl rhythm

PIHpihpih PIHpihpih PIHpihpih PAH
BIHbihbih BIHbihbih BIHbihbih BAH

TIHtihtih TIHtihtih TIHtihtih TAH
DIHdihdih DIHdihdih DIHdihdih DAH
KIHkihkih KIHkihkih KIHkihkih KAH
GIHgihgih GIHgihgih GIHgihgih GAH
KIHkihkih KIHkihkih KIHkihkih KAH
GIHgihgih GIHgihgih GIHgihgih GAH
TIHtihtih TIHtihtih TIHtihtih TAH
DIHdihdih DIHdihdih DIHdihdih DAH
PIHpihpih PIHpihpih PIHpihpih PAH
BIHbihbih BIHbihbih BIHbihbih BAH

b lamb rhythm

pa**Pop** pa**Pape** pa**Peep** pa**Pope** pa**Poop**
ba**Bob** ba**Babe** ba**Beeb** ba**Bobe** ba**Boob**
ta**Tot** ta**Tate** ta**Teet** ta**Tote** ta**Toot**
da**Dod** da**Dade** da**Deed** da**Dode** da**Dood**
na**Non** na**Nane** na**Neen** na**KNown** na**Noon**
la**Lol** la**Lale** la**Leel** la**Lole** la**Lool**
ka**Kok** ka**Cake** ka**Keek** ka**Koke** ka**Kook**
ga**Gog** ga**Gage** ga**Geeg** ga**Goge** ga**Goog**

Sentences for plosive practice

1 Harper performed happily at Peter's party.
2 Petunia, stop swapping your purple crop top.
3 Bob quibbled with Deb about her bubbly at the pub.
4 Fibbing in an autobiography is a blatant book betrayal.
5 Pre-pandemic, bobbing for apples was the best bet for swapping spit at a block party.
6 It's beneficial to balance prim repartee with ribald clapbacks when prattling with snobs.
7 Tom tickled Tatiana's tiny toes.
8 Ted took too much time to attach the carpet.
9 Dan drove down the driveway in a drowsy daze.

SPLASHING IN THE RIVER

10 Dentists defer to orthodontists when the patient's teeth are misaligned.

11 Derrick's stupendous dinner parties depended on plenty of meat.

12 I've told David time and again, "Don't diminish the pride of your aptitude."

13 Carrie's customers are coming in to look like Kim K.

14 Baking cookies kills countless seconds you can't get back.

15 Greg's green goggles got gunky in the bog.

16 The vegan guard dog grazed the August grass.

17 Killer gremlins wreaked havoc on Green Acres.

18 Can gum get stuck in the digestive tract of my cat or dog?

19 Paul and Brenda broke up because of his uncompromising tuba practice.

20 Pick a couple bunches of thyme from the garden.

Tongue twisters for plosive practice

1 paper poppy, paper poppy, paper poppy, paper poppy
baby bubble, baby bubble, baby bubble, baby bubble
paper poppy baby bubble, paper poppy baby bubble, paper poppy baby bubble.

2 Topeka, Topeka, Topeka, bodega, bodega, bodega

Topeka bodega, Topeka bodega, Topeka bodega, Topeka bodega.

3 Peter Piper, the pickled pepper picker, picked a peck of pickled peppers.

A peck of pickled peppers did Peter Piper, the pickled pepper picker, pick.

Now, if Peter Piper, the pickled pepper picker, picked a peck of pickled peppers,

Where is the peck of pickled peppers that Peter Piper, the pickled pepper picker, picked?

4 A big black bat flew past.

A big brown bat flew past.

Did the big black bat fly past faster than the big brown bat flew past?

5 "Sing a Song of Sixpence," English nursery rhyme

Sing a song of sixpence, a pocket full of rye.

Four and twenty blackbirds baked in a pie.

When the pie was opened, the birds began to sing.

Wasn't that a dainty dish to set before the king.

6 Jack Sprat would eat no fat,

His wife would eat no lean.

But together both,

They licked the platter clean.

Taps

A **tap** is formed when an articulator snaps to another articulator and releases without completely stopping the flow of air. This action feels different from a plosive, where two articulators touch, pause briefly to build air pressure, then release. A tap is more like a whipping motion.

Play: Whip it

Inhale through an open mouth, and as you exhale, bring different articulators together in a whipping motion, without allowing the pressure to build up behind them. Then try it with voice.

English doesn't have any *phonemic* taps or flaps. That means that the use of a tap instead of another sound does not change the meaning of the word. That being said, depending on the dialect of English, alveolar taps are used as allophones of "T," "D," or "R." This is the "T/D" sound in the New York City catchphrase "Fuhgeddaboudit," or the "R" in the Glaswegian "worm." To find this sound, hold out an "ah" and quickly whip the tip of your tongue up to the alveolar ridge and then back down. The resulting sound might be spelled "atta" or "ara."

Idiolectsploration: Taps

Read the following list of words while listening to and feeling for the underlined sound. Mark each word with [ɾ] for the alveolar tap, [d] for a "D" sound, [tʰ] for an aspirated "T," [t] for an unaspirated "T," [ʔ] for the glottal plosive, or ? for something else.

bi<u>tt</u>er___ bi<u>dd</u>er___ Ka<u>t</u> always___ The para<u>de</u> is___
pe<u>t</u>unia___ pe<u>d</u>antic___ abili<u>ty</u>___ be<u>d</u>azzle___
Ka<u>t t</u>alks___ Rei <u>d</u>oesn't___ cres<u>t</u>___ pe<u>d</u>ant___ fla<u>t</u>___

Do you notice any patterns? Does word stress change which allophone is used?

Read the following list of words while listening to and feeling for the underlined sound. Mark each word with [ɾ] for the alveolar tap or ? for something else.

th<u>r</u>u___ ca<u>rry</u>___ <u>r</u>ip___ the ca<u>r</u> is___ bo<u>r</u>ed___ t<u>r</u>ack___ po<u>r</u>ch___
talk<u>er</u>___ wo<u>r</u>ld___ hea<u>r</u>ing___ ai<u>r</u>ed___ health <u>r</u>isk___

Are you noticing any patterns? Do you pronounce each of the underlined sounds in the same way, or do you have different allophones of "R" that we've yet to explore?

Nasals

A nasal consonant occurs when the flow of air and vibration is blocked from escaping the mouth by the closure of two articulators while the pathway out of the nose is open. To open the nasal passage, the velum, or soft palate, lowers away from the wall of the nasopharynx. Let's find the movement of the velum. For this next exercise you may want to have a mirror handy so you can see the back of your mouth.

Play: Velum awareness

1   Watch the back of your mouth in a mirror. It's sometimes helpful to use a flashlight.

2. With your mouth open, inhale and exhale through your mouth. Make sure that no air is escaping your nose by placing one finger under your nose and feeling for warm breath.

3. With your mouth open and the tip of your tongue on your lower teeth, breathe through just your nose. Notice what moves in your mouth and nose in order to switch from mouth breathing to nose breathing.

4. With your mouth open, breathe in through your nose and out through your mouth, then in through your mouth and out through your nose. Notice the movement inside your mouth and nose that changes the path of the air.

5. Take a deep breath and hold it without closing your mouth. While holding your breath, imagine that you are about to breathe in through your mouth, allowing the articulators to move accordingly. Then imagine that you are about to breathe through your nose and let the articulators move accordingly.

6. Take over the action and choose to move your tongue and the velum toward and away from each other on purpose.

Play: Velum in action

1. Raise the velum by starting on an unexploded "B" /b/ sound. Voice will fill your mouth like you're about to cartoon vomit.

2. Then instead of exploding the /b/ out of your mouth, explode it out of your nose. That is the feeling of the velum dropping.

3. Now let's reverse that. Say (or sing) "MMMBop" in slow motion. The velum is lowered for the "MMM" and raises to turn "MMM" into a "B."

English has three nasal phonemes in the consonant inventory: the bilabial nasal, /m/; the alveolar nasal, /n/; and the velar nasal, /ŋ/. These sounds are fairly exclusively spelled with "M," "N," and "NG" or "NK." While these sounds are most commonly pronounced in their obvious placements, in certain accents of English, these nasal phonemes may be pronounced differently depending on what other sounds are near them. When these sounds shift, they usually move to the placement of the consonant that comes next. Take the word "onion," for instance. While I think of this word as starting with the syllable "un," I often pronounce this word as "UNG-yun," because the "N" sound moves from the tip of my tongue to the middle of my tongue, where the "Y" sound is created. This change is called **nasal assimilation** and it's so normal that it encoded itself in the English language for words like "bank" or "stink." Let's see if you have any nasal assimilation in your idiolect.

Idiolectsploration: Nasal assimilation

Speak the following phrases with a partner or on a video recording to see and hear if the nasal phoneme assimilates to the placement of the following consonant. Try speaking each sentence with assimilation and without. This skill will be important for future accent work, and avoiding assimilation may be the ticket if a director asks you to "enunciate" more.

1. Labiodental: Mo<u>m</u> <u>f</u>ound To<u>m</u> <u>f</u>unny. (Assimilation here means the "M" is pronounced on the upper teeth instead of the top lip.)

2. Alveolar: Runni<u>ng</u> <u>d</u>oesn't give me breathi<u>ng</u> <u>t</u>rouble. (Assimilation here means the "NG" is pronounced the same as "N.")

3. Bilabial: Ja<u>n</u> <u>b</u>akes te<u>n</u> <u>b</u>rownies. (Assimilation here means the "N" looks like an "M.")

4. Palatal: Ca<u>n</u> <u>y</u>ou climb in the ca<u>ny</u>on? (Assimilation here means the "N" is pronounced with the middle of the tongue, not the tip.)

Is nasal assimilation a part of your idiolect? If so, which consonants are affected?

Idiolectsploration: Vowel nasality

In some accents, nasal consonants will also affect the surrounding vowels because the velum drops before the start of the nasal consonant or lifts after the consonant has finished. In the IPA, this vowel nasality is described with /˜/ above the vowel. Speak the following phrases and decide if you hear or feel any nasality in the vowels. Sometimes it helps to pinch your nose and try to speak normally. If your voice changes, there's nasality trying to get through. If that change happens on a sound other than a nasal consonant, add /˜/ above the letters.

1   When I plan on going swimming, I want time to warm up beforehand.
2   I'm never sinking a pontoon again!
3   Mom warned me when I went under the sink that it might not be draining.

Do you hear any nasality in your vowels? Does it occur around all the nasal consonants, or just certain ones? If you hear nasality in the vowels, are they becoming nasal before nasal consonants, after, or both before and after?

For some accents, it will be important to reduce or increase the amount of nasality in the vowels. This can be done by changing the height of the velum during the vowel sound. To have more nasality, you can lower the velum to open the pathway to the nose. For less nasality you can raise the velum to close off the pathway to the nose. Read each of the preceding sentences two more times each, alternating between more nasality in the vowels (aim for that honking sound when your nose is pinched) and less (think of yawning while you speak). Whichever one feels easier to you is likely closer to your vocal tract posture.

Idiolectsploration: "NG"

Some accents of English will realize the "NG" sound as just a velar nasal consonant /ŋ/, and some will realize this sound as the nasal plus a velar plosive consonant, /ŋg/ or /ŋk/. Record the following and note next to each term whether you hear /n/, /ŋ/, /ŋg/, or /ŋk/.

fling___   Ming is___   hanger___   singing___
rang out___   strong___   thing___

Once you can tell which version you perform habitually, play with all three pronunciations. They'll be useful for future accent work.

Exercise: Nasal practice

1   Release your jaw using the exercises under "Exercise: Release" in Chapter 5. The following should be completed with a relaxed jaw.

2. Isolate your lips with blotting. Hold the taut edge of a clean piece of paper to your lip corners. Blot your lips on the paper and release without gripping in your jaw. Try blotting harder and harder without gripping or closing your jaw.

3. Release your jaw open wide enough to fit one finger between your molars from the outside of your cheeks. Hold your fingers there.

4. Isolate your tongue by firmly pressing the tip or blade to the alveolar ridge without biting down on your fingers (ten times).

5. Isolate your velum by saying "NGK" like the end of the word "rink." Notice what it feels like in your mouth when the air stops leaving your nose. Now try going back and forth between "NG" and "K" without exploding the "K." When you get it, you'll be isolating the back of the velum, which closes the nasopharyngeal port.

6. Isolate the intervocalic velar nasals.

    a. Find the "NG" /ŋ/ sound, like the nasal sound in the word "song."

    b. Slowly slide from "NG" to "AH" and then back to "NG" without ever stopping the flow of air.

    c. Play with the moment when your tongue and velum separate. How smooth can you make this separation?

    d. Start at "NG" and quickly raise the velum (as if you're just breathing out of your mouth) and pronounce "AH." Make sure the flow of air never stops so you don't hear a "G" sound.

    e. Practice moving from "NG" to vowels by saying "Sing EE, sing IH, sing EH, sing AA, sing UH, sing ER, sing OO, sing AW, sing AH." Make sure the flow of air and vibration never hiccups between the "NG" sound and the vowel.

7. Activate: Say, "Singing ah," without taking a break between words. Then add more "ings": "Sing-ing-ing-ing-ah." Speed that up.

Sentences for nasal practice

1. Mushrooms make a yummy accompaniment for lamb.
2. My mallard may not make it to Hamburg by May.
3. Ken pawned Nora's necklace.
4. There were ten hens in the pen.
5. The king stinks at singing jingles.
6. Jing sang while hanging twinkling lights on string.
7. My kitten has never been stung to my knowledge.
8. Tommy donned a pink tank top in mid-November.

Nasal tongue twisters

1. Mama made me mash my M&M'S (four times).
2. I need not your needles, they're needless to me.
    For the needing of needles is needless, you see.
    But did my neat trousers but need to be kneed,
    I then should have need of your needles indeed.
3. A skunk sat on a stump and thunk the stump stunk, but the stump thunk the skunk stunk.
4. Excerpt from "The Walrus and the Carpenter," by Lewis Carroll

    "The time has come," the walrus said, "to talk of many things:
    Of shoes—and ships—and sealing-wax—
    Of cabbages—and kings—
    And why the sea is boiling hot—
    And whether pigs have wings"
    …
    "O Oysters," said the Carpenter,
    "You've had a pleasant run!
    Shall we be trotting home again?"
    But answer came there none—
    And this was scarcely odd, because
    They'd eaten every one.

Trills

A **trill** is formed when an active articulator is braced up against a passive articulator as air moves through, causing a released part of the active articulator to wave and repeatedly touch the inactive articulator. Think of a flagpole! The pole is the inactive articulator and the flag is the active articulator. Part of the flag connects to the flagpole and is held taut while the end of the flag ripples in the breeze. This is exactly how speech trills work. Trills are continuous—not a repeated gesture, like repeating a series of "Ds." Most accents of English lack trills, but they're important to some accents, so we'll practice them here.

Exercise: Finding a lip trill /ʙ/

1 Bracing—activate your buccinator muscles to hold your lip corners tightly together.

2 Relaxed contact—let your lips gently touch one another. Don't press. The only work should be in the buccinators.

3 Flow—blow a fast stream of air at your lips. Let the lips ripple as air passes through.

4 Voicing—blow a stream of voice at your lips. Let the lips ripple as air passes through.

Exercise: Finding a tongue trill /r/

1 Bracing—brace the sides of your tongue to your top molars by saying "yee, yee, yee."

2 Relaxed contact—raise the tip of your tongue to the alveolar ridge like you're going to say "tee." Don't press. Let the tip stay relaxed.

3 Flow—blow a fast stream of air at the back of your tongue while holding the bracing.

4 Voicing—blow a stream of voice at your tongue while holding the bracing.

Alternate route

1. Put your tongue up like you're going to say "dee" but don't explode the plosive. Feel the sides of your tongue on the top molars. /d̄/
2. Try to keep the bracing of the / d̄ / in place while allowing air to pass between the tip of your tongue and the alveolar ridge.
3. Ease the pressure holding the tip of your tongue to the alveolar ridge while sending air and voice through. Don't lose the bracing!

Idiolectsploration: Trill out

Do you trill when speaking English? Speak the following sentences and note if you're trilling any of the underlined phonemes. Remember, a trill will have at least two instances of the active articulator touching the passive articulator. If it only has one, it's a tap. If there's audible friction, it's a fricative.

Voiced bilabial trill [B]: <u>B</u>obbie <u>b</u>roke <u>B</u>arry's ri<u>b</u> <u>b</u>oxing in <u>B</u>rixton.
Alveolar trill or voiced uvular trill [r, R]: To<u>r</u>y <u>wr</u>apped th<u>ree</u> wa<u>r</u>ped <u>r</u>ibbons a<u>r</u>ound T<u>r</u>isha's <u>pr</u>esent.
Voiced alveolar trill or voiced uvular trill [r, R]: Ma<u>r</u>k ma<u>rr</u>ied Mo<u>r</u>gan at a ch<u>ur</u>ch nea<u>r</u> the fi<u>r</u>e to<u>wer</u>.

Fricatives

A **fricative** is formed when air is passed between two articulators while they are being held close enough together for the turbulence, or friction, of the air to be audible. Fricatives are the most abundant sound in world languages, and there are more fricatives in English than any other manner of articulation.

Play: Finding fricatives

1. Inhale through an open mouth and release the air slowly while bringing different articulators together until you hear audible friction. Experiment with how close your articulators must be in order to hear the audible friction. If your articulators get close enough to form a seal and you feel pressure building behind them, you've gone too far and you're in plosive land.
2. Repeat the exercise with voice.
3. Place your hand on the outside of your mouth. Try to keep a stream of air blowing on your hand as you explore this exercise.
4. Do you recognize any of these sounds as English speech sounds?

English includes eight fricative phonemes in cognate pairs: "F" and "V," like in the words "fine" and "vine"; voiceless and voiced "TH," like in the words "thigh" and "thy"; "S" and "Z," like in the words "sip" and "zip"; and "SH" and "ZH," like in the words "shone" and "genre." The stand-alone phoneme "H," like in "hello," is also a fricative made with air passing through the vocal folds.

Idiolectsploration: Fricatives

Different accents of English treat fricatives in differently. Some accents may create a fricative with different articulators than expected, like pronouncing "think" with the sound commonly described as an "F" sound. Other accents might pronounce a voiceless phoneme at the end of words instead of their voiced counterparts. Record yourself reading the following word list. Listen and feel for which two articulators touch for each of the underlined sounds and whether the sound is voiced or voiceless. Feel free to use the IPA chart definitions of the different placements (see Figure 5 on page 111) to help you describe which sound you're actually using.

[f] voiceless labiodental fricative [v] voiced labiodental fricative
[θ] voiceless dental fricative [ð] voiced dental fricative
[s] voiceless alveolar fricative [z] voiced alveolar fricative
[ʃ] voiceless post-alveolar fricative [ʒ] voiced post-alveolar fricative

[h] glottal fricative [ʂ] voiceless retroflex fricative
[ʐ] voiced retroflex fricative ? something else

fairly____ muffin____ huff____ varied____ private____
stove____ thick____ Ethel____ bath____ thus____
mother____ bathe____ should____ usher____ wash____
genre____ massaging____ rouge____ haste____ ahead____
I told him so____

Sibilants are fricatives that are set apart from the others because of their hissing or shushing quality. This quality is created by a groove or channel down the center of the tongue that focuses the air into a thin stream. The resulting air friction is both louder and higher in pitch than that of other fricatives. "S," "Z," "SH," and "ZH" are all sibilant fricatives.

Play: Sliding sibilants

1 Make a "SH" sound.

2 Notice the shape of your tongue inside your mouth.

   a Notice the relationship between the sides of your tongue and your molars.

   b Where is the tip of your tongue? What is it pointing toward and how far away is it from that structure?

3 Keeping the tip of your tongue the same distance from the hard structures, slowly move the tip of your tongue forward until it's pointing at the back of your teeth, then slowly move the tip until it's pointing to your bottom teeth. Listen to the pitch changing.

   a Now draw it back to your top teeth, then as far back as it goes on your palate, and listen to the pitch change.

   b At what point do you move from the "SH" sound to the "S" sound and back again?

   c Can you feel and hear where your own "S" and "SH" sounds are created?

4 Repeat steps 1–3 while adding voice.

a Notice that the pitch of your voice and the pitch of the friction can change separately from each other.

b At what point do you move from the "Z" sound to the "ZH" sound and back again?

Idiolectsploration: Sibilants

Draw the shape of your tongue for each of the sounds in Table 6.

TABLE 6 *Idiolectsploration of Sibilants*

"S" like "sa<u>ss</u>"	"Z" like "<u>z</u>oo" or "ja<u>zz</u>"
"SH" like "shoe" or "a<u>sh</u>"	"ZH" like "<u>g</u>enre" or "massage"

Exercise: Fricative practice

1 Release your jaw using the exercises under "Exercise: Release" in Chapter 5. The following should be completed with a relaxed jaw.

2 Release the muscles of your tongue with a professional yawn.

3 Release your tongue with a massage under your chin.

4 Isolate the muscles of your upper lip by raising your lip to show your teeth (ten times).

5 Isolate the muscles of your tongue root by advancing your tongue out of your mouth and then relaxing it back behind your teeth.

6 Isolate the muscles of your tongue by bracing the sides of your tongue against your molars (ten times).

7 Isolate the muscles of your tongue by curling your tongue tip toward the back of the alveolar ridge without retracting the root.

8 Explore [f] and [v] by bringing your bottom lip to your upper teeth and sending air through that space. Listen for audible friction.

9. Explore /θ/ and /ð/ by gently touching the blade of your tongue to your upper front teeth. Send air through that space and listen for audible friction.
10. Explore /s/ and /z/ by imitating a jazzy high-hat cymbal, "SSS ts tss, SSS ts tss," and jazzy bumble bees, "ZZZ dz dzz, ZZZ dz dzz."
11. Explore "SH" and "ZH" by sending air through the groove toward the back of the alveolar ridge without extra tension.
12. Explore /h/ by easily whispering an "AH." Can you do this without tightening your jaw or pharynx muscles?
13. Activate your fricatives by speaking the nonsense phrases in Table 7, Fricative Clusters. Don't pause between words, but move directly from the first underlined fricative to the second without stopping the flow of air.

Sentences for practice

1. Philly feels fine in the fall.
2. Fred is daffy for Duffy.
3. Marv visited a groovy cave.
4. Vanya bravely advanced on Pavel.
5. We'll be very flabbergasted when Victor wins first place in the runoff.
6. Following every detail is difficult when Vince is woefully vague.
7. Catherine thought lethargy was deathly.
8. Authors bequeath thespians with Elizabethan teeth.
9. These moths dither on weathered leather.
10. Heather blathers without breathing.
11. The thing about breathing is that it'll help you coordinate thoughts.
12. Moths bathe in thimbles for their health.
13. Sam was sad that Sally sat beside Sue.
14. The soggy sandwich sat sopping in messy sauce.

TABLE 7 *Fricative Clusters*

		Second phoneme							
		f	v	θ	ð	s	z	ʃ	ʒ	H
First phoneme	f	if friends	laugh very	half think	if they	laughs	rough zoo	gruff shield	if Jacques	life help
	v	have fun	give veggies	brave thinker	have they	love some	Marv's	leave Sheila	have jus	live happily
	θ	math fiend	Ruth visits	Beth thinks	booth that	bath salts	death zap	Seth shakes	myth genre	youth hum
	ð	soothe Fred	bathe Viv	breathe thoughts	with that	eth symbol	seethes	breathe shakily	soothe Zsa Zsa	breathe hard
	s	less frantic	kiss villains	purse theft	bless thy	wasps sting	surface zit	grass shoot	lists genres	Boss hiccup
	z	has food	views vice	Liz thought	has that	brews some	Chaz zips	says she	thaws jus	booze hog
	ʃ	niche field	devilish villain	shush Thelma	push them	dish soap	plush zafu	wash shoes	hush Jacques	fresh jicama
	ʒ	beige feelings	prestige vacuum	beige thoughts	zhuzh that	massage school	mirage zingers	rouge shop	barrage Zsa Zsa	luge haul

15. Lazarus rose with razzle-dazzle and pleased his fans.
16. Liz, a business whiz, supervises the magazine.
17. Medusa zapped passersby into stone with mesmerizing snakes.
18. Desi was a snazzy dresser, a jazzy singer, and an astute producer now with commodes as his namesake.
19. Shaggy cushions shed shreds of shabby tissue.
20. Josh was shocked when Masha showed him the microfiche.
21. Jacques is so bougie he zhuzhed at the Taj Mahal.
22. Raj treasures prestige, not division or derision.
23. She said the dress code was casual and you showed up with an azure corsage.
24. You should know, few Persian rulers in Western Asia were actually called "shah."
25. Have Henry and Harriet had hamsters?
26. His healing has helped him have happiness.

Tongue twisters

1. A fly and a flea in a flue

    Were imprisoned, so what could they do?

    Said the fly, "Let us flee!" "Let us fly!" said the flea.

    And they flew through the flaw in the flue.

2. Whatever valley Wesley visits

    Verily welcomes his private wishes.

    He waits for the reverb then quietly leaves

    Vowing to wait for the dreams that he weaves.

3. Theophilus Thistle, the successful thistle sifter,

    Sifted sixty thistles through the thick of his thumb.

4. The lips, the teeth, the tip of the tongue.

    The tip of the tongue, the teeth, the lips.

5. Amidst the mists and coldest frosts,
   With stoutest wrists and loudest boasts,
   She thrusts her fists against the posts,
   And still insists she sees the ghosts.
6. Harry hushed his horse today,
   Who hurt his hooves by kicking his hay.
   Harry helped his horse heal, from his hungry ordeal,
   And happily hurried him back out to play.
7. Sally sells seashells by the seashore.
8. Selfish shellfish, selfish shellfish, selfish shellfish.

Affricates

We're going to step away from the IPA chart for a moment, because English includes two phonemes that are a special combination of two manners of articulation. **Affricates** are formed when a plosive is directly followed by a fricative. This close combination feels and sounds like it's all one movement, so speakers experience affricates as one distinct sound. In English, we have two affricates in the phonemic inventory: "CH" as in "church," and "J" as in "judge." Both of these affricates are a combination of an alveolar plosive with a post-alveolar fricative. "CH" is created with the combination of "T" exploding immediately into the "SH" sound, while "J" is the combination of "D" exploding into "ZH."

Play: Inventing affricates

Pick any plosive from the first column and any fricative from the second column. Pronounce these sounds in three ways: one alone and then the other alone (e.g., "T" then "SH"); one into the other (e.g., "TSH"); as one sound, an affricate (ex: "CH"). When creating affricates, remember they're quick sounds—no longer than a match strike.

"P"	"F"
"B"	"V"
"T"	"S"
"D"	"Z"
"K"	"SH"
"G"	"ZH"

Did you recognize any of the affricates you created? Some of these combinations will be easier to create an affricate with than others. Is there something about the placement of sounds that changes the relative ease or difficulty for you? Is there something about the voicing that changes the relative ease or difficulty?

Idiolectsploration: Affricates

Hopefully, you just felt the subtle difference between speaking a plosive followed by a fricative, and combining them to create an affricate. Play with the following words and phrases. For each of the underlined phonemes, decide if you hear and feel a plosive alone, a fricative alone, an affricate, or a plosive followed by a fricative. You can describe your answer in words, or you can use the IPA notation in the key. Remember, even though you may not expect an affricate in a word, you may still be pronouncing one even if it's not a phoneme in English.

Key:

plosives /t, d, p/   fricatives /ʃ, ʒ, f, s/
affricates /t͡ʃ, d͡ʒ, p͡f, t͡s, p͡s/ tap /ɾ/

[t], [ʃ], [t͡ʃ], or [t ʃ]: ca<u>tch</u>er_____   ca<u>sh</u>ier_____   ca<u>t sh</u>irt_____
   <u>tr</u>y_____   <u>t</u>une_____
[d], [ʒ], [d͡ʒ], or [d ʒ]: ba<u>d J</u>acques_____   a<u>z</u>ure_____
   bu<u>dg</u>et_____   <u>dr</u>ip_____   <u>du</u>ke_____
[mf], [mp͡f], or [mpf]: ca<u>mpf</u>ire_____   ca<u>me f</u>or_____   co<u>mf</u>y_____
   <u>Pf</u>eiffer_____
[t], [s], [t͡s], [t s], or [ɾ]: Pa<u>tt</u>y_____   Pa<u>ts</u>y_____   Pa<u>t s</u>aid_____
   la<u>ss</u>o_____   <u>ts</u>unami_____
[p], [s], [p͡s], or [p s]: sto<u>p s</u>aying_____   na<u>ps</u> are_____   cro<u>ps</u>_____
   <u>ps</u>ychology_____

Exercise: Practice sentences for affricates

1. Chad chewed his chimichurri chicken.
2. Cheese and ketchup are an unnatural match.
3. Junior was adjudicated by a regional magic jury.
4. I'll have a smidgeon of congealed vegemite.
5. Jack changed Charlie's jam-coated pajamas.
6. Judges challenged Shangela about her satchel dress.

Tongue twisters for affricates

1. Chicken kitchens, chicken kitchens, chicken kitchens.
2. Jane judged John's jump.
3. Charley chose to join the search,
   For children who marched into the birch.
   He checked far and near, then let out a cheer,
   When on a hunch he found them at church.
4. Jane was jolly she was chosen to judge,
   The championship match for makers of fudge.
   She tasted the chews, then encouraging news:
   Jellied ginger had won and she just wouldn't budge.

Approximants

Continuing our tour of consonants on the IPA chart, we're going to skip ahead to the approximants row. **Approximants** are voiced sounds created when two articulators move close together, with just enough room to avoid audible friction, and then glide apart. English includes two, three, or four approximant phonemes depending on the dialect. There might be an "R" like "round," "Y" like "you," "W" like "wood," and in some accents "WH" like "why." If the articulators were to move any closer together, you'd hear a fricative, and if they don't get close enough or if they hold still, you'll hear a vowel.

The "WH" phoneme, /ʍ/, is technically a voiceless fricative, but I'll include it here since it shares features with /w/. I've also seen that sound described as the "HW" sound, /hw/ instead of /ʍ/. Is that sound in your phonemic inventory? If so, would you describe it as an "H" followed quickly by "W" /hw/ or as all one sound /ʍ/?

Play: All the approximants

Find as many voiced fricatives as you can and slowly move the articulators away from each other until there is no audible friction—that is your starting point. Then quickly move to any vowel.

Bonus play: aWareness

"W" /w/ is an approximant, but there is no bilabial approximant listed on the pulmonic consonant chart. Can you feel something else happening in your mouth to create that sound? Try to find a "pure" bilabial approximant and go back and forth between that and /w/. What articulator do you feel behaving differently? Can you describe that difference? If you have the "WH" sound in your inventory, play with that as well. After you've explored how it feels, find the description of /w/ or /ʍ/ in the "other symbols" section of the IPA chart. Does that description match the feeling?

Idiolectsploration: "Y"

The placement of the body of the tongue in relation to the palate is what defines this phoneme. Read the following words and phrases out loud and decide whether you hear and feel an approximant, a fricative, or two vowels next to each other. Sometimes, an approximant "Y" will slip in between an "EE" and another vowel spoken in succession. This might happen in the middle of a word, or even between words.

Key:

approximant /j/   fricative /ʝ/
yellow___   YES!___   being___   froyo___
he only___   see you___   may I___   fire___

Idiolectsploration: "W" and "WH"

In some dialects of English, words spelled with "WH" may use the fricative /ʍ/ sound. Read the words and phrases below out loud and decide whether you hear and feel an approximant, a voiceless fricative, a voiced fricative, or two vowels next to each other. Sometimes a "W" will occur between an "OO" vowel and another vowel in the middle of a word or between two words.

Key:

voiced labial-velar approximant /w/
voiced bilabial fricative /β/
voiceless labial-velar fricative /ʍ/
something else ?

will___   WHY! ___   how is___   booing___
which___   witch___   go out___   power___

Exercise: Approximant practice

1 Release your jaw using the exercises under "Exercise: Release" in Chapter 5. The following should be completed with a relaxed jaw.

2 Release the muscles of your tongue with a professional yawn.

3 Release your tongue with a massage under your chin.

4 Activate the muscles of your lips by pursing your lips together (ten times).

5 Activate your tongue by pretending to scrape peanut butter off the roof of your mouth with the middle of your tongue.

6 Activate the middle of your tongue by touching it to the roof of your mouth (ten times). The tongue tip can stay relaxed down.

7 Energize your articulators by smoothly and quickly speaking the following:

   a OO-EE, OO-EE, OO-EE, OO-EE
   b OO-AW, OO-AW, OO-AW, OO-AW
   c OO-EE-OO-AW, OO-EE-OO-AW, OO-EE-OO-AW, OO-EE-OO-AW

d EE-OO, EE-OO, EE-OO, EE-OO

e EE-AW, EE-AW, EE-AW, EE-AW

f EE-OO-EE-AW, EE-OO-EE-AW, EE-OO-EE-AW, EE-OO-EE-AW

Sentences for approximant practice

1. Y'all, you're being yucky.
2. The youth are playing in the yard.
3. Why swim with whacky weasels?
4. Ewoks whine when Wookies wave weapons.
5. The bewhiskered whelp whimpered sweetly.
6. When waiting for Maryann's sourdough, we're watching yeast eat.
7. The viola solo I hear Joy is playing tomorrow is based on a swan crying.

Tongue twisters for approximant practice

1. Whether the weather is cool,
   Or whether the weather is hot,
   We'll be together, whatever the weather,
   Whether we like it or not.
2. There once was a woman of Shard,
   In younger years she went as a bard.
   She yells in her ire, "You're playing with fire!"
   Still, yon youths always play in her yard.

Lateral fricatives

There's a row in the pulmonic consonants section of the IPA chart with very few symbols in it, called **lateral fricatives**. **Lateral** sounds are formed when a spot on the midline of the tongue is held to another

SPLASHING IN THE RIVER

articulator, while the sides of the tongue do not create a seal. This sends the airflow over the sides of the tongue instead of over the tip. A lateral fricative is created when the sides of the tongue are held close to the teeth, so the lateral airflow creates audible friction. Lateral fricatives can be voiced or voiceless. English doesn't have any phonemic lateral approximants, but we'll explore them here to continue our work of differentiating fricatives from approximants. Readers who are also Welsh speakers may recognize the voiceless lateral fricative as the "LL" sound in Welsh.

Play: Freeform lateral fricatives

1 Touch the tip of your tongue to the alveolar ridge and breathe in. Feel the cool air moving over the sides of your tongue.

2 Draw the tip of your tongue backward along the centerline of the roof of your mouth to wake up your awareness.

3 Touch different sections of the centerline of your tongue to different sections of the centerline of the roof of your mouth. Make sure you can inhale in each new position.

4 Repeat step 3, but send breath through each shape so you can hear and feel the friction.

5 Repeat while sending voice through each shape.

6 Explore how close the sides of your tongue need to be to your teeth in order to hear the friction.

If you're having trouble hearing audible friction ...

1 Whisper an "L." If you don't hear much, move to step 2. If you hear audible friction, you're there already!

2 Slowly move from a whispered "L" to an unexploded "T" /t̚/ as if whispering "Halt."

3 Explore the "LT" in "Halt" in super slow motion.

4 Pause when you hear audible friction in the "L" and hold it out. That's the voiceless lateral fricative.

5 Send voice through that shape. That's the voiced lateral fricative.

Lateral approximants

Now that you've explored creating friction over the sides of the tongue, we can explore creating an approximant sound there. A **lateral approximant** is formed when a spot on the midline of the tongue is held to another articulator while sending the airflow over the sides of the tongue instead of over the tip. It is different from a lateral fricative because the sides of the tongue are relaxed away from the teeth, creating no audible friction. In English, we have one lateral approximant in the phonemic inventory, "L," but depending on your dialect of English, you might pronounce "L" with one, two, three, or four different sounds! Let's explore your "Ls."

Play: Making lateral approximants

1. Touch the tip of your tongue to the alveolar ridge and breathe in. Feel the cool air moving over the sides of your tongue.

2. Draw the tip of your tongue backward along the centerline of the roof of your mouth to wake up your awareness.

3. Touch different sections of the centerline of your tongue to different sections of the centerline of the roof of your mouth. Make sure you can inhale in each new position. How silent can you make that inhalation? How noisy can you make it?

4. Repeat step 3, but exhaling through each shape instead of inhaling. Toggle between a lateral fricative and a silent exhalation.

5. Repeat while sending voice through each shape.

6. Explore how relaxed the sides of your tongue must be to move from the lateral fricative to the lateral approximant.

Idiolectsploration: "L"

This section is a doozy and will take a bit of time. If it's too much for you right now, be more general with your exploration and come back to your "Ls" when and if your curiosity brings you back. It's never too late to learn more about your speech.

Record yourself reading the following word list. Pay close attention to the underlined sounds as you complete the prompt that follows.

leaf__ love__ loaf__ bowl__ bold__ below__
believe__ black__ pluck__ all out__ all over__

1. Compare the "L" sounds in each word and decide how many different pronunciations of "L" you have.
2. Mark all the words with "Ls" that are similar to the "L" in "leaf" with the number 1.
3. Assign the next number to every new "L" sound you find and label all the words that use that "L" with that number. You'll likely have between one and four "L" sounds in your accent, but I'm open to surprises if you are!
4. Draw the shape of your tongue for each "L" in Table 8. Notice the tip, sides, and back of your tongue for each "L."
   a. Is there contact with other articulators? If so, what section of your tongue contacts which articulator(s)?
   b. Inhale through your "L" shape. Sometimes the cool air can help you see or feel the shape of your tongue in your mind's eye.
5. Are any of your "L" sounds fricatives?
6. If your tongue isn't touching any part of the centerline of the roof of your mouth, that means that "L" is a vowel. Do you have any vowel "L" sounds?

TABLE 8 *Idiolectsploration of "L"*

1.	2.	3.	4.	5.

The pronunciation of "L" might change because of the types of sounds that are around it. In my accent I have four "L" sounds: (1) before front and central vowels (in my accent that's "leaf," "love," "black," "believe," "all out"); (2) after a vowel but before a consonant ("bold"); (3) after "t," "p," or "k" ("pluck"); (4) before back vowels or when the "L" is the last sound of a thought ("loaf," "below," "all over," "bowl"). The word list I've created includes all these variables. It also takes "L" in between two vowels and "L" in between words into account. Do your best to try to identify some of the "rules" for your different pronunciations of "L." List your rules for each "L" in the box above each drawing. It may be useful to look back at your idiolectsploration of lexical sets to see where in your mouth you pronounce the vowels. If you're really on a roll you might want to come up with words or phrases with "Ls" before or after each consonant to see if the "L" is affected. You can get creative.

Exercise: Practice for "L"

1. Release your jaw using the exercises under "Exercise: Release" in Chapter 5. The following should be completed with a relaxed jaw.
2. Release the muscles of your tongue with a professional yawn.
3. Release your tongue with a massage under your chin.
4. Activate your tongue tip by touching the tip of your tongue to the alveolar ridge and releasing it (ten times).
5. Energize your "L" sounds with the following:
   a lippity-pippity, lippity-pippity, lippity-pippity, lip
      libbidy-bibbidy, libbidy-bibbidy, libbidy-bibbidy, lib
      lippity-pippity, libbidy-bibbidy, lippity-pippity lip
      libbidy-bibbidy, lippity-pippity, libbidy-bibbidy, lib
   b luh-LAHL, luh-LAYL, luh-LEEL, luh-LOWL, luh-LOOL

Sentences for practice

1. Lisa lived in Clifton Knolls until college.
2. Cal was dealing lithium for moolah.
3. Ollie and Callie played Solomon with their dolly.

SPLASHING IN THE RIVER 175

4 Larry slathered lavash with licorice jelly for Mel.

5 I can tell, the lovers' dalliance belonged in Las Vegas.

Tongue twisters

1 Will you William? Will you William? Will you William? Will you William?

2 brilliant Italian William, brilliant Italian William, brilliant Italian William.

3 red leather, yellow leather, red leather, yellow leather, red leather, yellow leather.

4 Little Lonnie had a fall,

   While playing little league basketball.

   His neglected lace,

   Made him land on his face,

   And Lonnie lost the game after all.

Syllabic consonants

Until now we've been discussing the nucleus of syllables as vowels. There are situations, however, when a consonant can be the nucleus of a syllable, or a **syllabic consonant**. In order to be a syllabic consonant, the consonant must be a voiced consonant with no audible friction. "N," "M," and "L," are the most common syllabic consonants in English.

Let's look at one of my sticky-wicket words from my training, "gluten." The second syllable, "ten," is unstressed and ends with "N." How do you pronounce this syllable? It could sound like "ten," "tin," "tun," "in" (with a glottal plosive), or "tn," a syllabic "N." Play with it.

To perform a syllabic "N," there needs to be no vowel between the "T" and the "N," so the tip or blade of the tongue is going to stay put on whatever articulator it contacts for the "T." In my case that's the tip of my tongue on the alveolar ridge. In order to hear a "T," there needs to be an explosion. My tongue is going to stay in the same place to perform the "N" sound, so the velum drops and the air can explode out of the nose instead of the mouth in an action called **nasal release**. You can release a plosive into any nasal consonant you want. This is how we get the pronunciation of "captain" that sounds like "cap'm." Try it!

Now let's look at the word "ladle." There's an "L" in the unstressed syllable. For the "L" to be a syllabic consonant, there can't be a vowel between it and "D." The front of the tongue stays connected to the secondary articulator—in my case the tip of the tongue on the alveolar ridge—and in order to hear the explosion, the sides of the tongue drop away from the top molars, letting the explosion out over the sides of the tongue in an action called **lateral release**. Try it slowly with "ladle."

In some accents, you may even hear a syllabic consonant if the first syllable of a word is unstressed and includes one of these consonants. Take the word "important." Before drama school, I didn't pronounce the first syllable with a vowel. I started this word with a syllabic "M" and then moved into the rest of the word: "mportant."

Idiolectsploration: Syllabic consonants

Record yourself speaking the following words. Listen and feel for if you're pronouncing a vowel or a syllabic consonant. If you're exploring the IPA, you can mark a syllabic consonant with a small vertical line / ˌ / underneath the consonant symbol. When you're done, try going back and forth for each word between a syllabic consonant and a vowel sound.

harden___ rotten___ Latin___ ardent___ smitten___ pardon___ couldn't___ giggle___ whistle___ gleeful___ fiddlehead___ apple___ fable___ pickle___ prism___ complain___ imagine___ something___ slap him___ American___

"R" roundup

Until now, we've been glossing over a fairly large can of worms. "R" sounds, like "L" sounds, are very susceptible to changes in their pronunciation based on what part of the syllable they're in and what sounds are around them. "R" sounds change so much that they're

SPLASHING IN THE RIVER

commonly pronounced as both consonants and vowels, often in the same accent. When looking for vowel and consonant "Rs," I first look at where in the syllable the "R" is. An "R" in the onset or coda of a syllable is pronounced as a consonant. If the "R" sound is the nucleus of a syllable it's a vowel. As a reminder, for an "R" to be pronounced as a consonant, two articulators will partially obstruct the flow of breath and vibration, while vowel "Rs" will just shape the vibration while adding **rhoticity**, also known as "r-coloring." To make matters even more exciting, some accents of English don't have any rhoticity in their vowels. Such accents without rhoticity in the vowels, like those from London or the New York City area, are called **non-rhotic** accents.

In this section, we'll explore how you pronounce your consonant "Rs" and then pinpoint whether your accent is rhotic or non-rhotic. Again, take your time going through this section. You may get to a point and decide that you've learned enough about your "Rs" to last a lifetime. That's perfectly acceptable. If your curiosity does take you further, go easy on yourself. There's always more to uncover about the sounds in your accent. You don't have to get it all on the first go. Let's jump in.

Idiolectsploration: Consonant "R"

Let's pinpoint the consonant you use in the onset of syllables. Record yourself reading the following words and then complete the prompts that follow.

rate_____ road_____ borrow_____ parry_____ brow_____ prow_____

1 Compare the "R" sounds in each word and decide how many different pronunciations of the consonant "R" you have.

2 Mark all the words with "Rs" that are similar to the "R" in "rate" with the number 1.

3 Assign the next number to every new "R" sound you find and label all the words that use that "R" with that number. You'll likely have one or two consonant "R" sounds in your accent. I have two consonant "Rs": one that I use after /t/, /p/, or /k/, like in the words "try," "pry," and "cry"; and one I use everywhere else when there's a vowel after an "R."

4 Use Table 9 to draw the shape of your tongue for each "R."

    a Notice the tip, sides, and back of your tongue for each "R."

    b Is there contact with other articulators? If so, which section of your tongue contacts which articulator(s)? If not, which section of your tongue is getting close to which articulator(s)?

    c Inhale through your "R" shape. Sometimes the cool air can help you see or feel the shape of your tongue in your mind's eye.

5 Describe the movement.

    a Consonant "Rs" might be approximants, fricatives, trills, or taps. Which of these feels the most like your "R" motion?

    b Label each drawing with the manner of articulation for that "R" in Table 9.

6 Are all your "R" sounds voiced?

7 Like "L," your "R" can change depending on what sounds are near it. Can you tell what "rule" causes each of your "R" sounds? Label each drawing with the "rules" for that "R."

8 Notice your tongue root while you're pronouncing these "R" sounds. When the tongue root is active, it pulls the tongue backward toward the back wall of the pharynx. Sometimes this can feel like a down-and-back motion as well. Is your tongue root active?

9 Now you know the placement, manner, and voicing of all your consonant "R" sounds. If you're exploring the IPA, find the symbol that most closely matches this combination. If you feel your tongue root pulling backward, you can use the "retracted

TABLE 9 *Idiolectsploration of Consonant "R"*

1.	2.	3.	4.	5.
Manner:	Manner:	Manner:	Manner:	Manner:

tongue root" diacritic. If your consonant "R" is voiceless, and there is no voiceless symbol readily available, you can put the "voiceless" diacritic underneath the voiced IPA symbol that coincides with your placement and manner.

Idiolectsploration: Rhotic or non-rhotic

Now that you've found your consonant "Rs," we can discuss some of the possibilities for "Rs" that appear after a vowel in words like "shirt," "faster," or "start." First let's decide whether we speak with a rhotic or non-rhotic accent. Record the following pairs of words and complete the prompts that follow.

comm<u>a</u>/calm<u>er</u>   p<u>e</u>dantic/p<u>er</u>dition
sof<u>a</u>/suff<u>er</u>   c<u>o</u>mpliant/c<u>ur</u>mudgeon

1. Go back and forth speaking the words in each pair.
2. Listen to the underlined syllables of each of these pairs.
3. If the underlined syllables in the same pair sound different, can you hear rhoticity in one of the words? Rhoticity might have a quality similar to the sound you would make first if you said, "run" in slow motion. Rhotic accents will have rhoticity in the underlined vowels of the second word and no rhoticity in the underlined vowels of the first word.
4. If you don't hear a difference, you're speaking either a non-rhotic accent or perhaps an accent that adds extra rhoticity where there is no "R" in the spelling. Do you hear the "r-coloring" from the first sound of "run"? If not, your accent is non-rhotic.

Idiolectsploration: How rhotic?

If your accent is rhotic, the next step is to discern whether the "R" in this position is a consonant or a vowel.

1. Say the word "shirt" and note how many syllables you pronounce. In my accent, "shirt" is one syllable.
2. How many phonemes do you pronounce in "shirt"?

3. Can you separate the nucleus of the syllable from the "R" sound? If the "R" sound is the nucleus, then you're likely pronouncing a vowel that you can hold out. If the "R" can be split off after the vowel, you're likely pronouncing a consonant.

I count three phonemes in the word "shirt" in my accent. In the onset, I have "SH," then an "ER" sound is the nucleus, and then I have a "T" in the coda. Because that "ER" is the nucleus of my syllable, I can hold it out forever, and my articulators are not obstructing the flow of air and vibration, I can tell this is a rhotic vowel sound.

Perhaps your pronunciation includes four phonemes. If you can separate the nucleus of this syllable from the "R" sound, you might be pronouncing a consonant "R" here. The onset would be the "SH," the nucleus would be some kind of vowel, and then the coda might be an "R" consonant followed by a "T." This kind of pronunciation is most common in accents that use a tap or a trill as the consonant "R," but any consonant "R" could be found here.

Idiolectsploration: Vowel "Rs"

Some accents will have multiple vowels of "R." These differences in pronunciation might be caused by differences in spelling, like in certain Scottish accents, or by differences in word stress, like in accents found in the Northeast of the United States. Record the following sets of words and then complete the prompts that follow.

stressed syllables: c<u>er</u>tain___   w<u>or</u>d___   b<u>ir</u>d___
    c<u>ur</u>d___   h<u>ear</u>d___   j<u>our</u>ney___
unstressed syllables: p<u>er</u>cent___ clam<u>or</u>___   Vi<u>r</u>ginia___
    c<u>ur</u>tail___   stand<u>ard</u>___

1. Compare the underlined vowels of the first row, labeled, "stressed syllables," to one another. If you hear or feel a difference, number each new vowel you hear.

2. Compare the underlined vowels of each word in the "stressed" row with each word in the "unstressed" row. If you hear or feel a difference, number each new vowel you hear.

3 If you've labeled everything as 1, then you don't have a distinguishable difference between your vowels of "R."

4 If everything in the stressed row is 1, and everything in the unstressed row is 2, then you differentiate your "Rs" based on word stress. You have one vowel of "R" for stressed syllables, and a different vowel of "R" for unstressed syllables.

5 If you have more than two vowels and each is represented in stressed and unstressed syllables, then your "R" vowels might be dependent on the spelling of the word.

In some accents, "R" vowels are used to create diphthongs or even triphthongs by moving from a non-rhotic vowel to a vowel of "R." Now that you've discovered your different consonant and vowel "R" situations, you're ready to finish exploring your vowel phonetics. Feel free to return to the vowel mapping exercise in Chapter 8 to explore the lexical sets that you skipped and describe them with your newfound awareness.

Linking-R

The term "**linking-R**" is used to describe a consonant "R" that is added between a vowel "R" and another vowel that follows it. Say the word "roaring." Are you saying, "ROAR-ing," "RAW-ring," or "RO-ring"? Try pronouncing all three versions. If you hear the syllable "ring" in your pronunciation, you're likely using a linking-R. I go back and forth between using a linking-R and not. I suspect that I didn't use linking-Rs until I learned to in drama school. In some accents, a linking-R might even be inserted over word boundaries, like in the phrase "for everyone." If you hear the syllable "REV" in that phrase, you're likely using a linking-R. If you don't hear "REV," you might be linking these vowels without a consonant in between, or perhaps you're adding a subtle glottal attack between them.

    My favorite part about linking-Rs is that they might be added even when there's no "R" in the spelling of the word, especially by speakers of non-rhotic accents. Take the sentence "The pasta is cooked," for example. Because these speakers pronounce the vowels in the comMA, THOUGHT, and FAther lexical sets the same way that they pronounce the letTER, FORCE, and START lexical sets, respectively, they may use a linking-R after non-rhotic vowels as well. That means we might hear, "The pasta ris cooked," or, "The paster is cooked." A linking-R where there's not an "R" in the spelling is sometimes called an **intrusive-R**.

Idiolectsploration: Linking-R

Record yourself reading the following words and phrases, paying close attention to how you link the underlined sounds. Describe how you link each word or phrase. I've included an IPA key if you're exploring the IPA.

Key:

alveolar approximant /ɹ/   retroflex approximant /ɻ/
alveolar tap /ɾ/   alveolar trill /r/   glottal plosive /ʔ/   something else ?

ea<u>rr</u>ing___   a<u>r</u>ea___   sh<u>ow</u>e<u>r</u>ing___   s<u>u</u>rety___

murd<u>er</u>ous___   f<u>or</u>ever___   p<u>eer</u> <u>i</u>nto___   squ<u>ar</u>e <u>i</u>nch___

<u>our</u> <u>i</u>nk___   s<u>ure</u> <u>i</u>s___   h<u>er</u> <u>u</u>mbrella___   f<u>or</u> <u>e</u>very___

Exercise: Releasing tongue root retraction

Take a moment here to notice how your tongue feels, especially the tongue root. If you're a person like me who pulls the tongue backward toward the back wall of the throat to create certain "R" sounds, you may be feeling fatigued in this area of the throat. As a speech professional, I try not to judge sounds in myself or other people, so I won't say that tongue root retraction in and of itself is a bad habit that needs to be kicked. I will say, however, that speaking doesn't have to be uncomfortable, and the very muscular way that I pronounced "Rs" in my idiolect fatigued me during performances, especially when I was singing. As you know from the anatomy chapter, the tongue root, pharynx, larynx, and jaw are interconnected by different groups of muscles, so finding ease in the tongue root could lead to more vibration in your voice. I offer the following sequence with an intention of ease and not as a way to change your accent. Take from this sequence what you feel is useful.

SPLASHING IN THE RIVER

1. Jaw release:
   a. Massage the temporalis muscles on the sides of your head from above your ears to your temples.
   b. Massage your masseter muscles.
   c. Place four fingers under each cheekbone and drag them down your masseters.
   d. Shake your jaw straight up and down to release it.
2. Lip activation:
   a. Massage between your upper lip / nose and your lower lip / chin.
   b. Massage your lip corners.
   c. Isolate the inner orbicularis oris to find the pursing action. Relax your jaw.
   d. Isolate the risorius muscle to find spreading action.
   e. Wiggle your jaw with your hands while spreading.
3. Tongue root:
   a. Plant the tip of your tongue to your bottom teeth and stretch the back of your tongue over your teeth.
   b. Lift and tilt your head back and draw a rainbow on the ceiling with your chin.
   c. Keeping your jaw released, press the tip of your tongue into the back of your lips like cleaning up after a soft tortilla.
   d. With a released jaw, trace your teeth with the tip of your tongue (inside, sharp edges, and outside).
   e. Release your tongue out over your lip.
      i. Say "ERRRR" without retracting your tongue back in.
      ii. Say a tongue twister, then repeat it with your tongue inside your mouth.
   f. Massage under your chin. Press your thumb under your chin and speak a vowel chain without pushing your thumb out:

- i "EE, IH, EH, AA"
- ii "OO, U, AW, AH"
- iii "EY, AY, OY, OH, OW"
- iv "EAR, AIR, OOR, OR, ARE, IRE, HOUR"

4 Tongue groove:

 a Find the hotdog bun cupping action in your tongue and release (ten times).

 b With your tongue in your mouth, use the hot-dog-bun shape to brace your tongue against your molars (ten times).

5 Front of tongue articulation:

 a Wake up your tongue by scratching it along your upper front teeth.

 b Using the tip and blade of your tongue:

  - i Release your jaw so there is space between your molars.
  - ii Scratch the tip of your tongue on your upper front teeth.
  - iii Touch the tip of your tongue to the alveolar ridge and release (ten times).
  - iv Keep the sides of your tongue braced on your molars and repeat step iii.
  - v Whisper twenty-five "T" sounds with the tip of your tongue.
  - vi Speak twenty-five "D" sounds with the tip of your tongue.

"R" sentences

1 Rick rose in the ranks around when Perry retired.
2 Sharon was wary of the greedy regent.
3 The ruler rarely dressed in ruching and rouge.
4 The rural juror was ruthless to the wretched robber.
5 Jared gradually ran the prawn corral on the river.

Tongue twisters for "R"

1. Round the rugged rock the ragged rascal ran.
2. Red leather, yellow leather, red leather, yellow leather, red leather, yellow leather
3. Round and round the great arena,

    Race the Roman charioteers,

    Reckless of life, heedless of risk,

    Striving to gain that rich,

    and rare reward that men call fame.

10
MOVING FORWARD

You've just completed a detailed exploration of your own speech. That was a lot of work. Listen to your sample again. How do you feel about your speech now? Take a moment to think about some of the favorite things that you've discovered about your idiolect. Your favorite things will always be there for you. The gestures that feel really good when you employ them are useful tools for finding yourself in a writer's words. As you personalize the images, even the sounds that you use to create those words are full of history and context. You've moved your sounds from an accidental habit to a mindful choice that you can make every time you perform. That's huge. But now what? As the title of the book suggests, this was just an introduction to speechwork. From here on, you have choices about what to do with the information you've gathered about yourself and speech in general. Here are a few of the paths forward that I recommend.

Strengthening your idiolect

Now that you know what your accent is, the sentences for practice and tongue twisters will help you find speed and flexibility in your articulators. If a sentence like "Mama made me mash my M&M'S" is too difficult to say rapidly in your own accent, you can work on that. Speak the targeted exercises faster and faster until you can perform in your own accent at whatever speed a role could require of you. Another fun idiolect challenge is to go through the exercises with different degrees of articulation. What would a tongue twister feel like if you hit every consonant very hard? What if they were all very soft? When might you speak in such ways in your everyday life? Where on that spectrum is your usual, day-to-day conversational speech? Where along that spectrum are you best understood in your performance space?

Another spectrum you can explore is formality. Some people will code-switch to something they perceive as more fitting for a formal situation. "Formal" is subjective; it could mean speaking in public, speaking to an elder, or speaking to someone of higher perceived social status. Is this something you do? Perhaps there's a difference in your idiolect samples between the personal story you told and reading which might strike you as formality. Some people don't code-switch at all, which is also an exciting discovery. If you do notice formality differences in your speech, try speaking a few practice sentences at different points on that formality spectrum. Do you feel like this formality is part of your idiolect, or does it feel far enough away to be a different accent? In what situations in your life would you speak in this way? How does it make you feel to speak like that? Some actors will automatically switch to speaking with more formality when they're performing. Is this something you do? Do you mean or want to do it? If not, then practice performing in your idiolect with the words and sentences in each section.

Visiting your sources

Now is the perfect time to go back through the pages of this book and take a look at all your work. You've done a great deal of it. Your work represents something that is completely yours but at the same time connects you to your many communities. I highly recommend going through each chapter and rereading your notes for the idiolectsplorations. Now that you've explored all the sounds and built awareness of your vocal tract, you might discover something new about the sounds or how you use them in thoughts. Let's add yet another layer. Retrace your steps through the idiolectsplorations, and this time as you look over your work, think about where each sound or word or grammar specificity comes from. Do you get your unique "T" sounds from an individual or from one of your communities? Can you trace why they pronounce it like that? Who else in your life does that sound like? Whom does it distinguish you from?

At the end of that final idiolectsploration, you'll have a kind of map of your accent. It's a collection of all the people who have ever been important to you consciously or otherwise. Every time you have an impulse to speak, you gather the lessons that these communities have taught you while you take a breath and then turn your air and vibration into sense. I've found this idea quite profound. It has changed the way I judge the sound of my speech. In turn, my lack of judgment has opened me up to an even greater range of expression. I hope you will feel similarly. I hope your lack of judgment about your own sound will free you to draw on even more of your communities as you speak moving forward. Dig into the qualities you love so you can sound more authentically you, with all the strings attached.

Changing your speech

Part of accepting the specificity of your idiolect is knowing that it won't always be an appropriate choice for every role you audition for. I'm guessing that in your early career, it will be appropriate for most, but not all. Or you may be confronted, not quite with an accent request, but with a style request from a director or teacher. At one college I taught at, there was a professor with a vendetta against what she called "splashy Ts," and what I heard as "T" sounds made with the blade of the tongue, which created "S" aspiration, like "TS." She knew it was problematic to judge a sound so harshly, but she didn't like the sound of it coming from a Greek chorus. So, what do you do in one of these scenarios?

Start with the given circumstances of the character. Why are the sound changes necessary for the character? This is when you explore things like place of origin, languages spoken, places they've lived, approximate date of birth, race, ethnicity, socioeconomic class, education, sex, gender, sexuality, etc. These will pinpoint what accent you're looking for. If this is for a class or production, this step would definitely include a conversation with the teacher or the director. If it's for an audition, then sometimes casting will let you know what kind of accent if any to prepare. Sometimes, like in my Greek chorus example, the requested sound shift is less about the character and more about the style. Is it possible to create a reason that makes sense for the character? In the Greek chorus example, the actors decided that since the chorus was made up of the people of one city, they could all switch to a single pronunciation of "T," because it was the specific sound of that community. If you can't make sense of a requested accent for the character, then perhaps a more detailed conversation with the director is needed about the speech style and the reason it's being requested. Hopefully the answers will excite you to dive into the language in a different way. If the answers leave you feeling belittled or judged, then you should let the director know. You've done a lot of work learning about the sounds you use and where they come from and why they need to be respected. Feel free to use the specifics in your conversation. Knowledge is power.

Once you've gathered the given circumstances of the character, you can begin researching speakers. Try to find people who match your character's given circumstances as closely as possible. Everyone has an idiolect, so there's a little bit of wiggle room here. I start by researching people from the same location and then narrow that down by date of birth and then down the line. When I find someone who fits the bill, I see if there's an interview or speech of that person online. Sometimes, I'm lucky enough to be working on an accent for a community with an oral history project that has been uploaded to YouTube. If you're working with a director, you could share these videos with them to make sure that this is the accent they're hoping for.

Then comes the fun part. Watch, listen to, and respectfully mimic the videos. This is someone's idiolect. They have the same deep relationship with their communities that you do with yours. This is the sound of someone's parent or child. Treat this sound with the respect it deserves, so you can truly learn about it. If you're listening for one specific sound change, the job here will be easier. If you're changing your entire accent, then you have a lot more to do. Listen to the grammar for clues about how speakers of this idiolect put thoughts together. What words are they using in a special way? How are they using the musicality of their speech? What does your vocal tract feel like as you mimic their accent? What sounds do you hear that are different from your own? What stands out to you? At the end of this chapter, I've included a template for an accent breakdown that I would use to study a new accent for a project. As you explore this new accent, you can use something like that template to store your observations. It's just like exploring your own idiolect, as you've done over the course of this book, but now you can use your idiolect as a starting place. As you mimic the new sounds, you can compare them to your own. "I make my 'T' in this way, but for the new 'T' my tongue needs to move in this direction." Then record that in your breakdown. If you can't immediately mimic a sound perfectly, you're not alone! Just explore the sound you hear and the sound you make when you try to mimic it. Flip to that section of Chapter 9 in this book and remember some of the ways the vocal tract might be used differently to create that sound. Then explore changing how you use your vocal tract. You might have to subtly change the point of contact between articulators, or perhaps there's some assimilation happening, or even changing the manner of articulation. If you're working with vowels, remember that the sound is affected by the height of the arch or cup of the tongue, where that curve is in the front, middle, or back of the tongue, and lip rounding. Through exploring small changes, you will hear the target sound. Record how you got there.

Knowing what these speakers are doing is only the beginning of the work. The bulk lies in making the new accent a habit. Move one exercise at a time through the activate exercises in each chapter of the book. There are sentences and tongue twisters to practice each sound, and warm-up exercises to make changes to the shape of the vocal tract easier to accomplish. If there's a sound that proves more difficult to accomplish or to remember, then add exercises that target that sound to your daily warm-up. The goal of these drills is to find as much flexibility in this new accent as you have in your own. If it sounds like you're stuck in a repetitive musicality that's detached from the context of your thoughts, work on the prosody a bit more. There's likely a specific musicality for comparing things, for setups and spikes, for renaming, for negating, etc. Find them in your samples and practice them. You know you're performance-ready in an accent when you can go off script and improvise without ever dropping the accent. Try having everyday conversations in the accent without slowing down to think about it. Let yourself be led by real impulses and use the accent instinctively to get what you need. Taking on a new accent is a ton of work, but it can be a lot of fun.

Continuing your speechwork

If this book really excited you about speech, I highly recommend visiting all the materials in the Bibliography. Not only is there so much to learn, but often the same material taught by two different voices or in two different settings will strike you differently. You've explored speech through my personal filter, which I hope piqued your curiosity. If you're interested in applying more of a sense of play to your speech explorations, I highly recommend the "Experiencing Speech" and "Experiencing Accents" workshops, in that order, offered around the world by certified teachers of Knight-Thompson Speechwork. Some actors I know also work with private dialect coaches to build a repertoire of working accents that they can draw on quickly for auditions.

    Last, the best way to work on your speech is to be mindful of it as one thread in the tapestry that creates an actor. You can start by applying your speechwork to acting class or performance opportunities. You can also play with how speech sounds affect your voicework. Can you be aware of your speech and movement at the same time? Isn't your vocal tract part of your body anyway? How are you using your vocal tract while singing? How does your clown code-switch? Let the information you've gathered from your work here be present as you study the many other facets of being an actor. How has your awareness of your own speech changed the way you listen to others? How has it changed your awareness of judging others? I leave you with these questions, and I hope that they inspire more.

Appendix A
DAILY PRACTICE TEMPLATE

Use this template as a guide for building your personal practice. Pick one or two exercises for each box below. You can add more for areas that you need more work on. Repeat the same practice until you get bored of it and then change it up.

Release: Chapter 5					
Muscles of expression	Neck and throat	Jaw	Lips	Tongue	Velum

Isolate: Chapter 5						
Jaw	Lips	Cheeks	Tongue	Velum	Larynx and glottis	Pharynx

Activate: Chapter 5		
Tongue-ups	Tongue twisters	Connect to text

Prosody: Chapter 7			
Rhythm	Pitch	Pace	Volume

Phoneme practice: Chapters 8 and 9		
Words	Sentences	Text

Consonant clusters: Appendix C					

Appendix B
DIALECT BREAKDOWN TEMPLATE

1. Given circumstances

To pinpoint your accent research, fill in the following chart with everything the play tells you about your character's given circumstances. Quote the play and give a page number for each piece of definite information so you can easily find it in the future. If there is no definite mention of a piece of information, but there are clues, write those in the box without quotes. Leave boxes blank if no information is found. Missing information is up for discussion with the director and dramaturg.

Place(s) of origin / First language	Age / Approximate date of birth
Sex / Gender / Sexuality	Race / Ethnicity
Socioeconomic / Education Background	Places they've lived
Miscellaneous pertinent information	

APPENDIX B   195

2. People

Gather some research about the history of your accent and the people who speak it. Where did they come from? What do they do? What is their life like? Was this accent invented, was it an amalgamation of multiple languages coming together, or did it come about through isolation? Did this accent migrate? Think of the larger picture of your communities.

3. Vocal tract posture

1. Listen to and mimic your samples.
2. For each sentence you mimic, go back and forth between your idiolect and the accent.
3. Use Table 3 in Chapter 6 to observe the following characteristics of the accent one at a time. Be rigorous in your isolation of the parts.
4. Write down the characteristics as you identify them in your own mouth and body.

Description	Picture / Free association
Tongue:	
Lips:	
Jaw:	
Velum:	
Pharynx:	
Larynx:	

4. Prosody

1. Play your samples and move your body in response to one prosody feature at a time.
2. Describe the movement for each prosody feature in words and then draw a picture describing that feature.
3. Your observations here can be general; you'll add specifics in the next section.

Description	Picture
Rhythm	
Pitch	
Pace	
Volume	

5. Prosody and grammar features

1 Describe how the sample uses prosody to mark moving from one thought to another.

Description	Picture

2 Describe how the sample uses prosody to mark movement within the thought, like where the internal punctuation might be if the sentences were written.

Description	Picture

3 Describe how your samples use prosody as they organize thoughts in different sentence structures. These are the same sentence structures that you recorded yourself speaking in your sample. Describe the prosody you hear in words or a drawing. There are also blank spaces for you to add any others that you find interesting musically.

APPENDIX B

Structure	Example	Sentence from sample	Prosody description
Declaration	Joy had eight slices of pizza last night.		
Yes or no question	Do you want chicken for dinner?		
Open question	What is your favorite word?		
Command	Sit on the carpet.		
Negative command	Don't lose your purse.		
If/then statement	If we go out now, then we should stay in later.		
List of three+ items	I want to buy a shirt, slacks, and a tie.		
Multiple subjects	Mandy and Patti have been working together.		
Multiple verbs	I ate shellfish and had an allergic reaction.		
Independent clauses	I finished cleaning and Jack practiced violin.		
Dependent clause	When I was an actor, I hated tap dancing.		
Contrast	I have a red car, but you have a blue car.		
Parenthetical	Alistair (Jack's son) was late to school.		
Renaming	I had the best food ever: passionfruit.		

6. Lexicon

List the words that the sample speakers or characters use in a special way and define them. Include any words that are unfamiliar to you.

Word	Description / Definition
Canny	Pleasant or good (Newcastle, UK)
Jawn	Placeholder word for any noun except men or boys (Philadelphia)

7. Phonology

1 List the six phonemes that jump out at you the most and describe them. These can be vowels or consonants.

Phoneme	Sample word	Description	Notes

2. Find a phrase or two in your samples that includes as many of your key sounds as possible. Memorize it!

Phrase 1:

Phrase 2:

3. For a more detailed description of the accent, you can explore all the phonemes.

Lexical set	Description	Notes
FLEECE		
KIT		
DRESS		
TRAP		
BATH		
NURSE		
LETTER		
STRUT		

APPENDIX B

COMM**A**		
G**OO**SE		
T**U**NE		
F**OO**T		
OBEY		
TH**OUGH**T		
CL**O**TH		
L**O**T		
F**A**THER		
F**A**CE		
PR**I**CE/PR**I**ZE		
CH**OI**CE		
G**OA**T		
M**OU**TH		
N**EAR**		
SQ**UARE**		
C**URE**		
N**OR**TH/ F**OR**CE		
ST**AR**T		
ADM**IRE**		
P**OWER**		

Consonants

Phoneme	Example words	Initial	Medial	Final	Notes
"P"	pansy, dapper, lamp				
"B"	bee, cowboy, tube				
"T"	tree, bitter eat				
"D"	deer, meadow, pond				
"K"	coat, acre, freak				
"G"	go, bigger, fog				
"M"	mute, summer, am				
"N"	note, piano, noon				
"NG"	mango, singing	N/A			
"F"	friend, gaffer, life				
"V"	vamp, river, live				
θ	thank, Cathy, myth				
ð	the, wither, soothe				
"S"	see, festive, beasts				
"Z"	zeal, easy, jazz				
"SH"	shore, fashion, slash				
"ZH"	genre, version, beige				
"CH"	check, peachy, teach				
"J"	judge, Folgers, sage				
"H"	hello, mayhem				
"R"	rear, berry				
"L"	leer, belly				
"Y"	you, feud				
"WH"	where, somewhere				
"W"	wear, mowing, quiet				

APPENDIX B

Extra lexical sets

Lexical set	Description (IPA or height, place, rounding)	Notes

Appendix C
PRACTICE FOR CONSONANT CLUSTERS

Phoneme	Alone	+ɹ
p	peek, pill, pet, patch pay, pipe, pout, pork	prim, press, preen pry, prone, prowl
b	bean, bend, bat bay, bye, boy	brig, bread, brad bray, brow, bro
t	team, tick, tell, tomb, took, tock, tall, take	tree, trick, trend truth, trot, tray, tried
d	deed, din, debt, dash, dot, dumb, date, die	dream, drip, dress, drape, dry, drone
k	keep, kilt, Kelly, cook, coagulate, cay, coy	cream, krill, cringe, Cray, crime, crow
g	gi, gimlet, get, goop, good, gall, gods, gig	green, grip, grab, gray, grime, grown
f	fee, fill, fetter, foot, fall, fop, fame, fear	free, frill, friend, fray, fry, frown,
v	Venus, vicar, vet, vapid, verve, vomit	vroom
θ	theme, tick, thatch, enthusiasm, thyroid	three, threat, thrash, threw, throw, throat
s	see, sit, send, sat, sobriety, say, sigh	
sp	speech, spill, spell, spawn, spa, spud	spree, sprint, spread, sprung. spray, spry
st	steed, stick, stead, stall, stolid, stay, stye	street, strip, strength, strung, stray, stroll
sk	ski, skip, skeptic, Scott, scurvy, sky	screech, script, scrap, scribe, scroll, scrod,
sm	smith, smelt, smack, smock, smile, smoke	
sn	sneak, snitch, snack, snot, snail, snow	
sl	sleet, slim, slept, slump, slay, sly, slope	
ʃ	she, ship, shepherd, shawl, shun, shear	shriek, shrimp, shrub, shroom, shroud

APPENDIX C

+l	+j	+w
pleat, pluck, plat, plow, play, ply, ploy	pew, pure, Pyotr	
bleed, blip, bled, blade, blown, blight	imbue	
	*tune, tutor, tuba, tumor, tumult	tweak, twist, twill twain, twine, twenty
	*dupe, duty, duke, dune, due, duel	dweeb, Dwight, Dwayne, dwarf
clean, clip, clap, clay, Klein, clout	cue, cube, cure cucumber, peculiar	queen, quip, quack, quay, quiet, quote
glee, glint, glam, glow, glory, glower	ague, gyoza	penguin, Gwen, Guatemala, guac
flea, flint, fleck, flute, flurry, flood,	feud, funeral, fuel, fjord, few, fume	fois gras
	view, review	voila
		thwack
sleep, slid, slender, slack, slew, slaw, slop	*sue, consume, super, sewer	sweet, swill, sweat swoon, swan, sway
spleen, splint, splat, splay, explode	spew	
	stew, Kostya	
sclerosis, exclude, exclaim	skew	squeak, squid, squall, squab, squirrel, squat
	eschew	

Consonant clusters in the syllable coda

Phoneme	Alone	~l(c)	~n(c)
p p + "s" p + "ed"	cap, soup, lip laps, capes roped, duped	help, pulp Alps, yelps, gulped, helped	
b b + "s" b + "ed"	crab, rub, lob nibs, webs gabbed	bulb bulbs bulbed	
t t + "s"	let, boot, ate sits, oats	melt, guilt, cult belts, hilts	went, flint mints, pants
d d + "ed"	bed, rad, goad lads, buds	shield, build melds, wilds	band, find lands, kinds
k k + "s" k + "ed"	lack, tuck, ick licks, rakes puked, hiked	bulk, milk, ilk elks, sulks bilked, milked	*stink, skunk sinks, hunks linked, ranked
g g + "s" g + "ed"	rig, leg, cog bugs, bags lagged		finger, linger
m m + "d" m+"ed"	ham, loom palms, hems aimed, climbed	helm, film elms, realms overwhelmed	
n n + "s" n + "ed"	crone, lane pins, cranes, lined, coined	kiln kilns kilned	
ŋ ŋ + "s" ŋ + "ed"	sing, stung rings, wrongs fanged, winged		
f f + "d" f + "ed"	laugh, loaf cliffs, bluffs barfed, miffed	elf, self, wolf wolf's, engulfs engulfed	
v v + "s" v + "ed"	grieve, hive drives, saves craved, lived	valve, solve revolves shelved	
θ θ + "s" θ + "ed"	birth, myth maths, Earth's frothed	health, filth wealth's	tenth, synth months, ninths
ð ð + "s" ð + "ed"	bathe, loathe writhes, truths mouthed		

APPENDIX C

~m(c)	~s(c)	~(c)t	~(c)θ
lamp, stomp imps, stumps amped	asp, lisp, cusp gasps, wasps gasped	apt, inept erupts, tempts	depth depths
(The "b" is silent in final "mb" spelling)			
dreamt	list, paste mists, casts		
			width, breadth widths
	tusk, whisk discs, desks asked, risked	act, project, facts, sects	
		dreamt	warmth warmth's
	*lesson, fastens listened	rent, won't pants, hints	tenth, synth, plinth months, ninths
			strength lengths
lymph, nymph triumphs, triumphed		aft, bereft, rift lifts, sifts	fifth fifths
warmth warmth's			

Phoneme	Alone	~l(c)	~n(c)
s s + "s" s + "ed"	lass, grace passed, missed	else, false pulsed	hence, rinse, tensed
z z + "d" z + "ed"	rose, blaze sneezed		cleanse, lens cleansed
ʃ ʃ + "s" ʃ + "ed"	leash, mash hushed	Welsh	
ʒ ʒ + "ed"	beige, collage massaged		
t͡ʃ t͡ʃ +"ed"	latch, pooch matched	gulch, filch belched	bench, ranch punched
d͡ʒ d͡ʒ+"ed"	budge, dirge lodged, caged	bulge, bilge indulged	binge, grunge lunged, ranged
l l + "s" l + "ed"	reel, pool, foil pills, bowls tiled, nailed		*fennel, renal funnels tunneled
MISC (c) (c) + "s" (c)+"ed"	/ndθ/ thousandth thousandths	/ps/ apse, collapse collapsed	/mpt/ tempt attempts

Note: *a consonant cluster of these sounds would create a syllabic consonant.

APPENDIX C

~m(c)	~s(c)	~(c)t	~(c)θ
		feast, cast mists, frosts	
	*racism, prism chasms, isms spasmed		
		borsht borsht's	
*Dremel thermals enameled /dst/ amidst	*thistle hustles, jostles castled /lfθ/ twelfth twelfths	bolt, melt, silt belts, wilts	health, filth stealth wealth's

Appendix D
LIST OF COMPANION VIDEOS

To view any of the videos listed below, please visit **bloomsbury.pub/intro-to-speechwork**

- Release: Muscles of expression
- Release: Neck and throat
- Release: Jaw
- Release: Lips
- Release: Tongue
- Release: Velum
- Isolate: Jaw
- Isolate: Lips
- Isolate: Cheeks
- Isolate: Tongue
- Isolate: Velum
- Isolate: Larynx and glottis
- Isolate: Pharynx
- Activate: Tongue-ups
- Rhythm
- Pitch
- Pace
- Volume
- Moving mountains
- Vowel map

GLOSSARY

accent: The sounds of a spoken language. (p. 9)
adjectival phrase: A group of words that function together as an adjective, e.g., "The marbles *that fell on the floor* are blue." (p. 21)
adjective: A word or phrase that modifies a noun. (p. 18)
adverb: A word or phrase that modifies a verb. (p. 18)
adverbial phrase: A group of words that function together as an adverb, e.g., "I ran *as fast as lightning*." (p. 21)
affricate: A phoneme created by exploding a plosive directly into a fricative. (p. 165)
allophone: An individual pronunciation of a phoneme that has more than one pronunciation in the same accent. (p. 143)
alveolar: A consonant formed with tip or blade of the tongue and the alveolar ridge. (p. 141)
anapest: Two unstressed syllables followed by a stressed syllable, short-short-long. (p. 83)
approximant: A consonant created by two articulators held closely together, but far enough away to avoid audible friction. (p. 167)
article: A function word that introduces a noun, e.g., "a," "an," "the." (p. 25)
articulator: A part of the vocal tract used to create phonemes. Movable articulators change their shape to act on each other or on the immovable articulators, which do not change their shape. (p. 56)
aspect: Signals the degree of completeness in a verb, e.g., "She *is running*"; "She *had run*." (p. 19)
aspiration: Air from the lungs that delays the phonation of the following vowel or consonant. (p. 143)
assimilation: When a consonant sound changes its placement based on the sounds around it. (p. 153)
auxiliary verb: A verb used to indicate the tense or mood of another verb, e.g., "I *was* running." (p. 28)
bilabial: A consonant formed using two lips. (p. 141)
breathy voice: A vocal register where the vocal folds are held apart partially, allowing some phonation and some unphonated air to pass though. (p. 76)

cardinal vowels: The vowels created in even intervals, which correspond to symbols on the IPA chart. (p. 119)

clause: A phrase that has subject-verb agreement and is part of a larger sentence. (p. 23)

code-switching: Changing the language, dialect, or accent of speech. (p. 94)

cognate pair: Two consonants with matching placement and manner, but different voicing. (p. 142)

conjugation: When a verb changes its form to communicate person, number, tense, aspect, or mood. (p. 19)

conjunction: A function word that connects images or clauses in a thought, e.g., "*and, but, because, if, or,*" etc. (p. 25)

consonant: Phoneme created by obstructing the flow of air and vibration in the vocal tract using the articulators. (p. 114)

consonant cluster: A group of consonants spoken together as the onset or coda of a syllable, sometimes over word boundaries. (p. 96)

copulative verb: A verb that links an adjective back onto the subject, e.g., "I *am* hungry." (p. 28)

creaky voice: Also called vocal fry, this is a vocal register where slow air flow between the vocal folds makes the undulation of the vocal folds slower. The resulting sound is somewhat like a noisy door. (p. 76)

dactyl: A stressed syllable followed by two unstressed syllables, long-short-short. (p. 83)

definite article: A function word that introduces a specific singular or plural noun. (*the*). (p. 25)

dental: A consonant formed with the tip or blade of the tongue and the back of the upper teeth. (p. 141)

dependent clause: A phrase with subject-verb agreement that cannot form its own complete thought, e.g., "*When I ate pie*, I liked it." (p. 23)

diacritic: An IPA marking that notates a change in the sound of the base symbol. (p. 142)

dialect: A form of a language that differs from another form because of its accent and at least one other quality like grammar or lexicon.

diphthong: Two vowels spoken in a single syllable. (p. 9)

direct object: A noun in the verb phrase that receives the action of the verb, e.g., "I ate *apples*." (p. 20)

egressive: From the inside of the vocal tract to the outside of the vocal tract. (p. 114)

fricative: A consonant formed by two articulators held closely enough together to create audible air friction. (p. 158)

function words: Non-image words that organize images into grammatical relationships. (p. 24)

gemination: Lengthening a consonant for a longer duration than that of a single consonant. (p. 145)

gerund: An "-ing" verb form that is used as a noun, in either the subject or object of a thought. (p. 20)

GLOSSARY

glottal: A consonant formed with the vocal folds as an articulator. (p. 142)
glottis: The open space between the vocal folds. (p. 74)
grammar: The specific rules and structures of a language or dialect. (p. 9)
head: The main word of a phrase that is modified by the words around it, e.g., "My left *arm*." (p. 30)
iamb: Rhythm pattern of an unstressed syllable followed by a stressed syllable, short-long. (p. 84)
idiolect: An individual's accent, which encompasses their entire social location and may sound different from the people around them. (p. 4)
image: Parts of speech that we can close our eyes and imagine, remember, smell, or do. (p. 18)
imperative mood: Verb communicating a command, e.g., "Run!" (p. 19)
indefinite article: a function word that introduces a single, nonspecific member of a noun group (*a, an*). (p. 25)
independent clause: A phrase with subject-verb agreement that could form its own complete thought, e.g., "*I ate pie* and *I liked it*." (p. 23)
indicative mood: A verb communicating a fact as a declaration or question. (p. 19)
indirect object: A noun in the verb phrase that is affected by the verb but is not the direct object, e.g., "I threw *him* the ball." (p. 20)
infinitive: A verb form in the present tense preceded by "to." Infinitives can be used as nouns, e.g., "*To eat* was my only wish," or adverbs, e.g., "I want *to eat*." (p. 20)
ingressive: From the outside of the vocal tract to the inside of the vocal tract. (p. 114)
interjection: Exclamations and outbursts that lack any subject-verb agreement. (p. 24)
International Phonetic Alphabet: A collection of symbols used to notate the sound of speech. (p. 8)
intrusive-R: A consonant "R" added after a vowel when there is no "R" in the spelling. (p. 182)
labiodental: A consonant formed with the bottom lip and the upper teeth. (p. 141)
language: The words, structures, and rules we use in specific combinations to communicate. (p. 9)
larynx: The movable cartilage structure housing the vocal folds. Also known as the voice box. (p. 74)
lateral: A phoneme created by sending air and vibration over the sides of the tongue. (p. 170)
lateral approximant: A manner of articulation where the air and vibration travel over the sides of the tongue without creating audible friction. (p. 172)
lateral fricative: A manner of articulation where the air and vibration travels audibly over the sides of the tongue instead of the tip. (p. 170)
lateral release: The action of exploding a plosive over the sides of the tongue instead of over the tip of the tongue. (p. 176)

lexical set: A group of words spoken with the same vowel, used to compare accents. (p. 121)

lexicon: The particular vocabulary of a language or dialect. (p. 35)

linking-R: A consonant "R" added between an "R" vowel and another vowel. (p. 181)

manner of articulation: The mechanism by which a consonant is produced. (p. 142)

minimal pairs: Two words that share all but one phoneme; used to compare sounds. (p. 14)

modal voice: A vocal register where the air passing through the vocal folds makes them undulate against each other, which creates the vibration we hear as pitch. (p. 76)

modifier: A word or phrase specifying the meaning of another word, like adjectives or adverbs. (p. 21)

mood: Different verb forms used to express the speaker's attitude about what they're saying. Moods are used to express statements of fact, questions, commands, conditions, or hypotheticals. (p. 19)

mora-timed: Describes a language in which syllables are broken down into roughly even beats. (p. 98)

nasal: A phoneme that is created by sending sound and vibration out of the nose. (p. 151)

nasal assimilation: When the placement of a nasal phoneme changes to match the placement of the surrounding consonants. (p. 153)

nasal release: The action of exploding a plosive through the nose instead of out of the mouth. (p. 176)

negative: Function word that introduces a lack of the image it modifies, e.g., "no," "not." (p. 29)

no audible release: The action of stopping the flow of air in a plosive without the characteristic explosion of sound that follows. (p. 145)

non-pulmonic: A phoneme created without the use of air from the lungs. (p. 115)

non-rhotic: An accent that does not include vowels with rhoticity, or "R-coloring." (p. 177)

noun: Part of speech that corresponds to a person, place, thing, concept, etc., that could complete the action of a verb. (p. 18)

noun phrase: A group of words in a sentence that function together as a noun, e.g., "my kitten," "the blue house that I grew up in." (p. 20)

nucleus: The most vowel-like phoneme that makes up a syllable. (p. 95)

number: The singleness or multitude of the noun of the thought, e.g., "I *am*"; "We *are*." (p. 19)

object: A noun that is part of the verb phrase because it receives the action of the verb. (p. 20)

objective complement: A word that modifies, names, or renames the direct object of the thought, e.g., "This makes me *happy*." (p. 32)

GLOSSARY

operative word: A stressed word of a thought that conveys the meaning. (p. 21) **palatal:** A consonant formed with the body of the tongue and the palate. (p.142) **participial phrase:** A group of words beginning with a participle which acts as a modifier. (p. 19)
participle: The "-ing" form of a verb commonly used in conjugation to express tense, aspect, or mood, e.g., "I had been *running*." (p. 19)
parts of speech: Categories of words that behave in the same way, e.g., nouns, verbs, adverbs. (p. 18)
person: The point of view of the noun of a thought, e.g., "I," "you," "we," etc. (p. 19)
pharyngeal: A consonant formed with the root of the tongue and the pharynx. (p. 142)
pharynx: The back part of the nose, mouth, and throat used in breathing, eating, and speech. (p. 78)
phonation: The vibration of the vocal folds which creates vocal pitch. (p. 74)
phoneme: An individual speech sound. (p. 95)
phonemic inventory: The list of sounds used in an accent. (p. 121)
phonemics: The study of speech sounds in general without the details of pronunciation. (p. 121)
phonetics: The study of the actual realization of speech sounds in an accent. (p. 121)
phonology: The study of individual speech sounds and how they behave in a language. (p. 112)
phrase: Multiple words that form a single part of speech. (p. 18)
placement of articulation: The articulators involved in the creation of consonants. (p. 141)
plosive: Manner of articulation in which two articulators form a seal, stopping the flow of air and then move apart, creating a characteristic popping noise. (p. 143)
post-alveolar: A consonant formed with tip or blade of the tongue just behind the alveolar ridge. (p. 142)
preposition: A function word that shows a relationship between images; often spatial e.g., "to," "from," "on," "at," "with." (p. 26)
prepositional phrase: A group of words that begins with a preposition and functions as either an adjective or an adverb, e.g., "Let's go *to the fair*." (p. 26)
primary stress: The most prominent syllable of a word. (p. 96)
pronoun: A function word that takes the place of a previously introduced noun. (p. 26)
prosody: The pitch, rhythm, pace, and volume of speech. (p. 91)
pulmonic: A phoneme created using air from the lungs. (p. 114)
pyrrhic: Rhythm pattern of two unstressed syllables in succession, short-short. (p. 102)
retroflex: A consonant formed with the bottom of the tip of the tongue and the palate. (p. 142)

rhoticity: The quality of "R," or r-coloring in a vowel. (p. 117)
schwa: The vowel sound created by the lack of a curve in the tongue. (p. 119)
secondary stress: The second-most prominent syllable of a multisyllabic word. (p. 96)
sibilant: A fricative consonant created by sending air down a thin channel that creates a hissing or shushing sound. (p. 160)
social location: A person's demographic background, which forms the building blocks of the person's idiolect. (p. 15)
spondee: Rhythm pattern of two stressed syllables in succession, long-long. (p. 102)
stress: The use of prosody to make a syllable stand out from the rest of a word or sentence. (p. 45)
stress-timed: Describes a language that changes the length of syllables to make the time between stressed syllables roughly equal. (p. 98)
subject: The noun that does the action of the verb in a thought. (p. 20)
subjective complement: An adjective following a copulative verb and describing the subject as part of the verb phrase, e.g., "I am *hungry*." (p. 32)
subject-verb agreement: A verb conjugated in accordance with the person and number of its subject, the building block of a complete thought, e.g., "He runs." (p. 22)
subjunctive mood: Verb communicating something hypothetical, wishful, doubtful, or just not factual, e.g., "She wishes she *were running*"; "If she got up earlier, then she *would run*." (p. 19)
suprasegmental: The notation of speech features other than the component parts of a consonant or a vowel, e.g., pitch, length, or stress. (p. 142)
syllabic consonant: A consonant that acts as the nucleus of a syllable. (p. 175)
syllable: A pulse of sound energy that has a nucleus and may include consonants in the onset or coda. (p. 94)
syllable coda: The consonants of a syllable after the nucleus. (p. 95)
syllable onset: The consonants of a syllable before the nucleus. (p.95)
syllable-timed: Describes a language in which syllables take roughly the same amount of time to pronounce. (p. 98)
tap: A consonant sound formed by the quick contact of two articulators which do not stop the flow of air. (p. 150)
tense: Communicates time period in a verb, e.g., "She *runs*"; "She *ran*." (p. 19)
thought stress: The use of prosody to emphasize words and phrases over entire sentences. (p. 97)
trill: A continuous consonant characterized by the repeated contact between a relaxed articulator and another articulator. (p. 157)
triphthong: Three vowels spoken in the same syllable. (p. 120)
trochee: Rhythm pattern of a stressed syllable followed by an unstressed syllable, long-short. (p. 83)
unstressed: A syllable or word that is not emphasized in speech. (p. 96)
uvular: A consonant formed with the body of the tongue and the uvula. (p. 142)
velar: A consonant formed with the body of the tongue and the velum. (p. 142)

velum: The soft back section of the roof of the mouth which acts as an articulator by changing shape to connect or disconnect the oral cavity from the nasal cavity. (p. 72)

verb: Word(s) in the sentence that communicate(s) what the subject does. (p. 18)

verb of being: Any conjugation of "to be." See copulative verbs. (p. 28)

verb phrase: A group of words in a sentence that function together as a verb. (p. 19)

vocal folds: Also known as vocal cords, these are a set of two bands of muscle tissue in the larynx used for phonation. (p. 74)

vocal fry: *See creaky voice.* (p. 76)

vocal tract: The pathway in the throat, mouth, and nose that breath and vibration pass through to create human speech. (p. 87)

vocal tract posture: Habitual shapes of the muscles of the throat, mouth, and nose that help create a speaker's phonemic inventory. (p. 87)

voiced phoneme: A sound that is created including the phonation of the vocal folds. (p. 114)

voiceless phoneme: Phoneme created without the phonation of the vocal folds. (p. 114)

vowel: A voiced phoneme created with no obstruction of air and vibration by the articulators. (p. 114)

weak form: An unstressed pronunciation of a function word with a reduced vowel. (p. 25)

whisper: A vocal register where all sounds are voiceless, because the vocal folds are not in close enough proximity to phonate. (p. 75)

word stress: The use of prosody to make one or two syllables sound more important than others inside a word. (p. 9)

BIBLIOGRAPHY

Behrens, Susan J., and Judith A. Parker. *Language in the Real World: An Introduction to Linguistics*. London: Routledge, 2010.

Burns Florey, Kitty. *Sister Bernadette's Barking Dog: The Quirky History and Lost Art of Diagramming Sentences*. Hoboken, NJ: Melville House, 2006.

Carley, Paul, Inger Margrethe Mees, and Beverley Collins. *English Phonetics and Pronunciation Practice*. London: Routledge, 2018.

Catford, J. C. *A Practical Introduction to Phonetics*. Oxford: Oxford University Press, 2010.

Collins, Beverley, Inger M. Mees, and Paul Carley. *Practical English Phonetics and Phonology: A Resource Book for Students*. New York, NY: Routledge, 2019.

Gilroy, Anne M., Brian R. Macpherson, and Lawrence M. Ross. *Atlas of Anatomy*. Stuttgart: Thieme, 2008.

Gussenhoven, Carlos, and Haike Jacobs. *Understanding Phonology*. London: Routledge, 2017.

Hammond, David. "Talking Shakespeare: A Workshop." Lecture series at American Repertory Theater Institute at Harvard University, Cambridge, MA, 2011–14.

Houfek, Nancy. "The Five Floodgates." Speech, American Repertory Theater and Moscow Art Theater School Institute for Advanced Theater Training at Harvard University, MA, 2011.

Kapit, Wynn, and Lawrence M. Elson. *The Anatomy Coloring Book*. San Francisco, CA: Pearson, 2014.

Knight, Dudley. *Speaking with Skill: An Introduction to Knight-Thompson Speechwork*. London: Bloomsbury, 2012.

Mrthoth (Thomas Peyser). English Grammar Lessons (YouTube channel). https://www.youtube.com/channel/UCWXba4Y-xQI3DRTD0k45i8Q (accessed 2019–20).

Nordquist, Richard. "Definition and Examples of Major and Minor Moods in English Grammar." ThoughtCo., January 19, 2019. https://www.thoughtco.com/mood-in-grammar-1691405 (accessed November 17, 2020).

Saladin, Kenneth S., and Carol Porth. *Anatomy and Physiology: The Unity of Form and Function*. Boston, MA: WCB/McGraw Hill, 1998.

Skinner, Edith, Lilene Mansell, and Timothy Monich. *Speak with Distinction*. Edited by Lilene Mansell. New York, NY: Applause Theatre and Cinema Books, 1990.

Wells, Carolyn. *The Jingle Book*. New York, NY: Macmillan, 1899.

Wells, J. C. *Accents of English: An Introduction*. Cambridge: Cambridge University Press, 1998.

www.ingramcontent.com/pod-product-compliance
Lightning Source LLC
Chambersburg PA
CBHW071838230426
43671CB00012B/1993